T0071328

TAROT
FOR
SELF-CARE

~MINERVA SIEGEL~

HOW TO USE TAROT TO
Manifest Your Best Self

Adams Media
New York · London · Toronto · Sydney · New Delhi

DEDICATION

This book is dedicated to the magnificent multidimensionality of existing as a human being, because shrinking oneself to fit boxes and binaries is for the banal, bland, and boring. I dedicate this book to becoming less perfect, and more free, as self-care.

. . . .

Adams Media
An Imprint of Simon & Schuster, Inc.
100 Technology Center Drive
Stoughton, MA 02072

First Adams Media hardcover edition October 2019

ADAMS MEDIA and colophon are trademarks of Simon & Schuster.

For information about special discounts for bulk purchases, please contact Simon & Schuster Special Sales at 1-866-506-1949 or business@simonandschuster.com.

The Simon & Schuster Speakers Bureau can bring authors to your live event. For more information or to book an event contact the Simon & Schuster Speakers Bureau at 1-866-248-3049 or visit our website at www.simonspeakers.com.

Interior design by Julia Jacintho
Interior illustrations by Nicola DosSantos

Manufactured in the United States of America

5 2022

Library of Congress Cataloging-in-Publication Data
Names: Siegel, Minerva, author.
Title: Tarot for self-care / Minerva Siegel.
Description: Avon, Massachusetts: Adams Media, 2019.
Includes index.
Identifiers: LCCN 2019023004 (print) | LCCN 2019023005 (ebook) | ISBN 9781507210970 (hc) | ISBN 9781507210987 (ebook)
Subjects: LCSH: Tarot. | Self-actualization (Psychology)--Miscellanea. | Self-care, Health--Miscellanea.
Classification: LCC BF1879.T2 S54 2019 (print) | LCC BF1879.T2 (ebook) | DDC 133.3/2424--dc23
LC record available at https://lccn.loc.gov/2019023004
LC ebook record available at https://lccn.loc.gov/2019023005

ISBN 978-1-5072-1097-0
ISBN 978-1-5072-1098-7 (ebook)

Table of Contents

Chapter 5

Minor Arcana Interpreted **97**

Part 3: Optimizing Your Self-Care – 211

Introduction

At its core, self-care involves digging deep within yourself to create energetic balance in your life, recognize social and environmental conditioning that isn't serving you well, and embrace your truest self. Tarot can help you accomplish all of this—and more! You can:

- Use The Empress to strengthen your connection with the natural world.
- Use The Hermit to set healthy boundaries.
- Use The Chariot to promote confidence.

A marvelously versatile tool, tarot is about much more than turning over cards in a deck; it can be used to exercise your intuitive muscles, analyze yourself in constructive ways, and learn to own your potential.

Tarot for Self-Care is your complete, modern guide to reading tarot and using the cards in self-empowering, deeply fulfilling ways. Whether you are new to tarot or an advanced practitioner, you'll find unique and refreshingly nonbinary perspectives that look at the art of reading the cards through a lens inclusive to all genders. To this end, gender-neutral "they/their" pronouns are used throughout the book.

First, you'll learn how to prepare for tarot readings, from decluttering your mind to using tools such as energy-infused candles, tea leaves, and smoke cleansing to enhance the power of the tarot reading experience. You will also discover how to use a pendulum to check in with your chakras for an even deeper reading. Next, you'll dive into the cards themselves. Here, you'll discover the story of the major arcana and how to apply its meaningful lessons to everyday life, as well as methods for shuffling and drawing tarot cards, and how to arrange drawn cards into different tarot spreads. To help you understand the meanings of the individual tarot cards, we've also included detailed descriptions and interpretations of each of the seventy-eight tarot cards, written with unique self-care tips for every upright and reverse position.

Once you have mastered the art of reading tarot, you will learn how to make your readings vibe higher using crystals, before digging even more deeply into self-care to explore your shadow-self and specific areas where you may need to focus your self-care practices. These pages are full of creative and inspiring self-care tips and activities that encourage you to look within; check in with and align your energy centers; and nurture yourself in powerful, transformative ways. After all, self-care isn't *just* about face masks and indulging in a favorite luxury. (Although, let's be real: Those things are great too!)

Whether you're looking to make tarot part of a regular self-care routine, or you wish to use it as a more intermittent tool for personal growth, you'll find everything you need in *Tarot for Self-Care*. So dive in and get ready to explore your inner magic through tarot. After all, you deserve to live a happy and abundant life as the very best version of you that you can be!

Self-Care

Beyond the Buzzword

Self-care is *en vogue* and here to stay, and that's marvelous—but what *is* it, exactly? In the simplest terms, self-care is the practice of doing things for yourself with compassionate intent. Through self-care, you restore both mental and physical energy, nurture the wonderful traits and talents that make you who you are, and simply feel *good*. It can involve those little things you often hear about, like skincare routines and indulging in little luxuries that make you happy, but, at its heart, it's much deeper than that. The ultimate goal of self-care is to cultivate yourself comprehensively so you can become the brightest version of yourself. Unlearning toxic behaviors, recognizing the ways in which you can improve yourself, and taking care of your health are all major parts of self-care.

Through the magic of tarot, you will discover your own path for personal wellness, but above all else, remember that self-care is the best way you can show yourself love. After all, you need to love yourself just as much as you love other important people in your life.

Types of Self-Care

This comprehensive self-care can also be broken down into three main types that cover every aspect of your life. As you dive more deeply into the world of personal care, you will discover how each type can be tailored to your unique needs, and how tarot can act as a guiding light to the best self-care practices for you:

- **Mental Self-Care.** This involves any practices that restore or nurture the mind, including managing stress through a breathing exercise, cultivating creativity through an artistic hobby, and boosting your mood with a funny video. Mental self-care is important for managing your emotions, organizing and understanding thoughts, and succeeding in everything you do—from career ambitions to personal interests.

- **Physical Self-Care.** This involves any practices that restore or nurture the body, including getting enough sleep, working out, and eating a balanced meal. Your body is a temple, and physical self-care allows you to properly honor and nourish it.

- **Spiritual Self-Care.** This involves any practices that restore or nurture the spirit, including meditating, attending a worship service, and releasing negative energy through a Reiki session. Spiritual self-care is important for exploring meaning and connecting to the world around you, no matter your personal beliefs or values.

You might use a self-care activity to target one area that you feel is in need of a little extra TLC—like using the mental self-care practice of journaling to calm anxious thoughts during a stressful week at work—or you might weave activities within all three types into your daily routine. Paying attention to what aspects of your life need self-care and when will enable you to maintain balance and overall wellness, no matter what life throws your way!

Self-Care and You

It is also through practicing this care for your mind, body, and spirit that you celebrate your successes, learn from your missteps, and, most importantly, discover who you are at your very core. After all, when you really get to know yourself, you can reject the things that don't align with your best, happiest life. Rather than wasting time on thoughts, people, or practices that don't help you vibe higher, when you get to know and trust your truest self through self-care, you are better equipped to fill that space with the kinds of positive beliefs, relationships, and activities that deeply nourish you.

This is a lot to think about, I know, but luckily, the wonderful realm of tarot is here to help. Through these powerful, insightful cards, you'll soon be a pro at caring for your unique needs. So, are you ready to dive in? Let's begin!

PART 1
·············
THE ART OF READING TAROT

Whether you lean heavily into the spiritualism of tarot, approach this art from a more secular lens, or are picking up a tarot deck for the first time, reading tarot can provide you with an absolute wealth of personal insight. The cards are tools to help you access your subconscious mind. They encourage you to be analytical, and they help you view the situations you find yourself in more objectively. After all, it's often hard to see things practically when you're in the thick of it, so tarot can help you take a better look from different, unexpected, and beneficial perspectives. It encourages you to discover and acknowledge your most intrinsic truths—both positive and negative. Using these revelations, you can celebrate your light (the positive qualities that give you your signature *je ne sais quoi* and brilliant inner glow), recognize your shadow (any negative or problematic traits you hold), and discover which behaviors, conditioned responses, ideologies, and perceptions might not be serving you well. Reading tarot is an integral part of my own self-care regimen, and I'm excited to share with you how it's done!

Before we get into the deeper topics of using tarot for self-care, however, it's important that you have a fundamental knowledge of the tarot reading process. The following chapters will help you to get into the analytical and open mindset perfect for reading tarot, while also giving you lots of tips and activities for setting up your perfect tarot space along the way. And after learning how to prepare your mental and physical space for a reading, it will be time to dive into the particulars of the reading. Learning how to read tarot can seem intimidating at first, but never fear! I have lots of tricks to help you as you shuffle, draw, and arrange the cards.

Chapter 1

Set the Stage:
Methods for Manifesting a Magical Mood

While reading tarot doesn't always have to be a long process (hey, life gets busy sometimes!), taking the time to prepare for readings whenever possible will help you to connect fully with your inner magic. After all, the actual cards are just tools; the art of reading tarot is only as magical as you are. And (spoiler alert): You're *super* magical. Every person is magical, in fact, and the spiritual self-care you practice through tarot is a great way to tap into that magic and get it to work for *you*.

The following chapter is devoted to manifesting this magic in the most beneficial, powerful ways possible. Here, you will discover how to create a perfect space for reading tarot, including how to use items such as candles and smoke to aid in your ritual. Are you ready to unlock your magic?

Readying Your Mind for Tarot

Before you begin bringing different objects and scents into your tarot ritual, it is important that you ready your mind for the reading. An open, positive mental space is key for a truly beneficial tarot experience. You shouldn't go into the reading with many expectations, as the cards will rarely take you down a path you have anticipated. Instead, acknowledge the uncertainty ahead. After all, not knowing is part of the excitement of a tarot reading! Truly anything can happen. Once you have opened your mind to the possibilities and begun channeling the incredible energy of the ritual ahead, you will be ready to decorate your chosen space with whatever spiritual objects and scents you prefer.

Powering Up with Candles

One of the first items in your tarot space should be a candle or two—or five. Candles are perfect for signifying the beginnings and endings of tarot sessions. Great ones to use are called dressed candles. These have been anointed with oils, flora, or crystals, and sometimes carved with symbolic markings called "sigils." Dressed candles are infused with specific, magical intent, and many of them also feature aromatherapy benefits that enhance the tarot experience.

When performing tarot readings with very specific goals or themes in mind, use candles made with wax colors that correspond to the theme(s) of the reading. This helps invoke the right energy to get the best result. Here's a handy color reference chart:

COLORS AND THEIR MEANINGS	
Red	Passion, courage, romantic love
Pink	Self-love, friendship, partnerships
Orange	Action, self-esteem, creativity
Yellow	Friendship, happiness, intellectual pursuits
Gold	Money, wealth, power
Green	Healing, transformation, success, luck
Blue	Communication, calmness, clarity
Purple	Clairvoyance, justice, spirituality
White	All-purpose, enhancing personal magic
Black	Divination, protection, overcoming obstacles
Silver	Psychic awareness, uncovering secrets
Brown	Security, nature magic, grounding energy

Using Sacred Smoke for Spiritual Cleansing

Smoke cleansing is another great way you can use the power of scent to prepare your energy for a tarot reading. Different forms of smoke cleansing have been used in cultures all over the world for centuries. In Catholicism, censers filled with smoking incense are swung back and forth during some liturgical services. Smudging is a practice common in many indigenous cultures that involves burning plants (commonly sage) in an abalone shell and fanning the smoke with a feather. In recent years, people have often used the term "smudging" incorrectly to refer to the practice of simply burning sage. The actual act of smudging is a sacred indigenous ritual. If you're not of a culture that traditionally practices smudging, please use terms like "smoke cleansing" or "aroma cleansing" to refer to your own sacred smoke practice.

Smoke cleansing refreshes both personal energy and the energy of a room. It clears the auric field, and it rids a space of unwanted and/or negative energy.

SPIRITUAL SELF-CARE TIP: CLEANSING YOUR TAROT SPACE

It can be difficult to feel relaxed and ready for a tarot ritual in a messy space. When in chaotic, unorganized places, your energy can often reflect that environment. Infusing a cleaning routine with magical intent is a great way to prepare a ritual location for a reading—plus, it's just good spiritual hygiene. There are many ways to do this. You can:

- Play recordings of crystal singing bowls or other meditative sounds while you clean
- Use sage-infused cleaning products (sage is an energetically cleansing plant)
- Create a floor-washing solution with spiritually purifying essential oils such as lavender
- Burn magically dressed candles that feature uplifting essential oils

Spiritual Self-Care Activity: Smoke Cleanse with Sage

Smoke cleansing can also be used to cleanse residual energy from objects! You can smoke cleanse all secondhand objects that come into your possession to make sure they're filled with nothing but positive vibes. Use the following guide to smoke cleanse with sage:

Items Needed:
- A lighter or matches
- 1 bundle dried sage
- 1 small fire-safe container

Instructions:
1. Use lighter or matches to light one end of dried sage bundle in the fire-safe container.
2. Blow out the flame after a moment or two, leaving the end smoking steadily.
3. Walk around the room with the container of sage, making sure the smoke wafts into every corner.

You can also say protective prayers or chants while doing this cleanse. Here is one example: "Chase away things that cause fright. Leave only love. Leave only light." Perform this ritual weekly throughout your home as energetic maintenance. It can also be done when someone in the home is experiencing nightmares, after arguments, and before spiritual activities like reading tarot.

. . . .

Filling the space with a cleansing aroma will set the perfect tone for reading tea leaves, trying out a new tarot playlist, or performing any other practice you enlist to prepare your energy for a tarot reading. Be sure to explore different scents as you gain experience reading tarot to find out which ones are most helpful to you.

Tapping Into Tarot with Tea Leaves

There's nothing quite like sitting down with a cup of warm, perfectly steeped tea to manifest a calm, contemplative mood. This is the ideal mindset, coincidentally, for tarot reading. It's easier to view the cards' meanings more objectively and analytically when you're in a peaceful state of mind. To bring about this mental state, you can practice the art of tasseography, which is commonly known as reading tea leaves. Before a tarot reading, steep a warm cup of tea with magical intent and use it as divination. Many different kinds of tea can be used to enhance magical moods and prepare you for tarot interpretation. Here's a list of common teas and their magical associations:

- **Black Tea:** Expelling Negativity, Promoting Stability, Energy Grounding
- **Green Tea:** Emotional and Spiritual Healing, Love, Transformations, Success
- **Oolong Tea:** Self-Reflection, Meditation, Concentration, Friendship
- **White Tea:** Happiness, Beginnings, Clarity, Cleansing Energy
- **Herbal Tea:** Magical properties depend on the herbs used—hibiscus is known for promoting self-love

Mental Self-Care Activity: Read Tea Leaves to Prepare for Tarot

The art of tasseography can help you access your intuitive mind, making it a great self-care practice to use before tarot readings. By enhancing your coming tarot reading with tea leaves, you will be better able to glean any messages of personal care, warning, etc. from the cards. There are many different "rules" for tasseography floating around in the world, so you should explore which variations are the best fit for you. Here is one simple way to read tea leaves:

Items Needed:

- 1 teacup or mug with a handle and saucer
- Hot drinking water
- Loose-leaf tea of your choice

Instructions:

1. Place loose-leaf tea in your cup and pour hot water over it.

2. As the tea steeps, place both hands on the cup and think about the intent behind this tea leaf reading.

3. Sip the tea slowly until there's only a very small amount left in the cup.

4. Focus on sending a burst of your energy into the cup as you swirl it thrice clockwise.

5. Place the saucer over the top and tip the cup upside down, and then tip it back up and place it in front of you with the handle pointing toward you.

6. Look inside the cup. What imagery comes to mind when you look at the remaining tea leaves? How do the symbols make you feel? Consider the placement of these symbols in physical relation to the rim and bottom of the cup. What part(s) of the cup feel intuitively like they tell of past events? Future events? Are the effects of these situations long-term or short-term? Keep the cup's imagery and messages in mind as you move forward into your tarot reading.

Using Music to Cultivate a Mystical Mindset

From lighting candles to observing tea leaves, stimulating all of the senses during any kind of spiritual activity can help you feel more present and connected to the act—so it's no surprise that listening to music is another important part of getting in the mood for tarot. Music is a great tool that can help you access the perfect state of mind for tarot reading. Play around with different genres! Notice how different kinds of music make you feel, and how those feelings translate to your interpretations of tarot spreads. Put together a playlist full of music that makes you feel sensual, and play it whenever you do tarot readings about love. Make another playlist with jams that pump you up, and use it to help you feel confident and powerful during readings on days when you're seeking guidance. During everyday tarot readings, listen to calm music that puts you in touch with your emotions.

Bathing As a Sacred Spiritual Ritual

Luxurious, soothing, and a perfect place to listen to those new tarot playlists, baths are great for spiritual self-care. Use this relaxing alone time to center your energy and rejuvenate your spirit by infusing your bath with a bit of magical intent. This will help to get you into the calm, meditative state of mind that's perfect for reading tarot.

. . . .

Physical Self-Care Activity: Get Clean with a Spiritually Charged Bath

Infusing your bathing routines with magical intent is a great way to prepare your energy for tarot readings. The following bath uses visualization exercises to clean and clear your aura, leaving you refreshed and ready for tarot, so you can better understand what self-care messages a reading is offering you. Feel free to follow it exactly, or to use it simply as inspiration!

Items Needed:

- Music
- 1 white candle
- A warm bath
- Your favorite spiritual cleansing tool, such as sage smoke

*Feel free to add bath bombs, bath salts, or any other bath additives that will personally enhance and customize the experience for you.

Instructions:

1. Play your chosen music to set the mood, and light the candle to signify the awakening of your magical consciousness.

2. As your bath fills with water, be still, and focus on the candle's flame while calling to mind the intent of the ritual. Think positive affirmations, for example: "I am magical. I am powerful. I am loved."

3. Next, energetically purify your space using your chosen method. For example, if you're using sage, light it in a fire-safe container and let its smoke gently waft around the room. When the bath is full, climb in, and let yourself lounge for a while. Enjoy the warmth and comfort of the bath.

4. When you're ready, wash your body while visualizing negativity sliding off of you as you scrub.

5. After you've scrubbed yourself down from head to toe, get out of the bath right away; don't linger in the spiritually dirty water. As you get out of the tub, take a moment to consider the water slipping down the drain, and visualize the negative vibes you washed off swirling away with it.

Ta-da! Now you're clean from crown to root chakra, as well as from head to toe!

. . . .

Showering can also be a great time for spiritual cleansing! One simple shower ritual involves visualizing the falling water as containing energetically cleansing white light. Close your eyes and imagine the water from the showerhead washing away all negative energy from you from head to toe. As bad vibes, anxiety, and fear disappear down the drain, imagine yourself being filled with brilliant, confident light.

And now that you're feeling relaxed and refreshed, it's time to get down to business: discovering the divine in the details of tarot!

Chapter 2

Find the Divine in the Details: A Crash Course on Interpreting Tarot

The standard tarot deck (known as the Rider-Waite deck) is made up of seventy-eight cards, which are divided into two groups: the major arcana and minor arcana. The twenty-two major arcana cards signify major life lessons with long-lasting impacts. The fifty-six minor arcana cards tell of day-to-day situations with short-term effects. The minor arcana are also divided into four suits: Cups, Wands, Swords, and Pentacles. Each suit has four court cards, which represent actual people or personality archetypes, and ten numbered cards which tell you about everyday situations, themes, and lessons. *Whew—that's a lot to think about!* Fortunately, there are two handy tools for better understanding these cards: The Fool's Journey and numerology. The Fool's Journey helps put the major arcana into perspective and makes remembering the cards a breeze, while numerology breaks the minor arcana down into ten distinct categories that are much easier to follow.

In this chapter, you'll join The Fool on this exciting trek through the major arcana. Note that The Fool and all of the other archetypes represented by the major and minor arcana can represent people of any gender, which is why I exclusively use gender-neutral "they/their" pronouns when describing this journey. After The Fool's Journey, you'll dive into numerology, followed by a more comprehensive look at the minor arcana suits. You'll also discover lots of little tips and tricks along the way to help you even more as you explore the deck!

The Fool's Journey to Enlightenment

The Fool's Journey tells the story of the very first card in the major arcana: The Fool. Numbered 0, The Fool starts out innocently, hopefully, and a little naïvely, on a trek through the major arcana, learning lots of lessons and meeting many important archetypal figures along the way. The Fool's ultimate goal is personal enlightenment. As you'll soon discover, this intense and adventure-filled journey through the major arcana has so much to teach you!

The Magician

As The Fool starts out on their path to enlightenment, the first person they meet is The Magician. A powerful, flashy conjurer, The Magician teaches The Fool about the importance of concentration and shows them how to manifest their innate talents through focus.

The High Priestess

After this meeting with The Magician, The Fool continues happily along the path and soon comes across another powerful figure: The High Priestess. Wise and regal, The High Priestess inspires The Fool to dig deep and listen to their inner instincts and intuition. "You have wisdom of your own," The High Priestess says serenely. "Explore it."

The Empress

Moving along, The Fool then encounters a beautiful, lovely figure lounging in a lush garden. This figure, The Empress, teaches The Fool to connect with their inner nurturing spirit. Tender-hearted, loving, and kind, The Empress inspires The Fool to appreciate the beauty of the natural world. "Every living thing deserves compassion," The Empress says, smiling, "and that includes you. Take care of yourself with love."

The Emperor

While still marveling at the beauty of nature, The Fool comes across the ruler of the land: The Emperor. This authoritative figure takes the time to teach The Fool about the importance of self-discipline, leadership, and organization.

The Hierophant

Counsel to The Emperor, The Hierophant then helps the wide-eyed Fool appreciate the value of time-honored traditions, organized structures, and established institutions.

The Lovers

By now The Fool has learned a lot of comprehensive, important lessons. While pondering them, The Fool runs into a potential life partner at a crossroads. Represented by The Lovers tarot card, the time spent with this potential life partner teaches The Fool about unions and partnerships. Before too long, however, The Fool realizes they are presented with a tough decision: to join up with this lover permanently, or to continue on the path to enlightenment alone. Eventually, The Fool decides that they need to resume their journey on their own, and, grateful for the experience, they continue along the path.

The Chariot

The Chariot is the next card in the major arcana, marking a time during which willpower is called for. A very triumphant figure, The Chariot now reminds The Fool that it's time to put their nose to the grindstone in order to reach the enlightenment they seek. "Don't give up," says The Chariot, "because victory is at hand. You are in control of your own life. Own your power!"

Strength

A lesson in Strength is next learned as The Fool journeys on and comes across a figure calmly taming a lion. The figure teaches The Fool to recognize the importance of steady perseverance and the power of a gentle touch when leading others.

The Hermit

Next, a solitary figure is seen illuminating The Fool's path with a single lantern. This Hermit teaches The Fool about the necessity of introspection and occasional solitude. This has been a very busy journey for The Fool so far, and there's a lot to reflect on. "Make time for yourself," The Hermit suggests softly.

MENTAL SELF-CARE TIP:
SET HEALTHY BOUNDARIES WITH THE HERMIT

Time alone is an essential part of mental self-care. Many people have busy, bustling lives, and making time for introspection can be difficult. Still, no matter how busy your life is, time alone to relax and recharge is a necessity. It doesn't need to be an extended period of time either; sometimes a few minutes is all it takes to feel restored, so work that time into your schedule on a regular basis. This may mean saying no to a social event, or cutting an unnecessary project from your calendar. Remember the lesson of The Hermit: Setting boundaries that help you create time to yourself isn't selfish—it's basic self-care, and you deserve it.

The Wheel of Fortune

After this introspective period, The Fool continues along the path and soon finds themselves in front of The Wheel of Fortune. Here, they realize the cyclical nature of life. This tarot card also represents sudden, positive changes, as well as good luck.

Justice

Skipping right along, The Fool begins to think about the concept of Justice. "What's right, and what's wrong?" The Fool asks themselves. The Justice tarot card comes into play here, stressing the importance of fairness, morality, and balance.

The Hanged Man

While still pondering Justice, The Fool rests precariously in a tree, and then slips. Hanging upside down from a branch and becoming The Hanged Man, The Fool realizes the value of looking at situations from new and unexpected perspectives.

Death

After righting themselves and climbing down from the tree, The Fool has a meeting with a rather imposing figure: Death. Death, though startling at first, isn't to be feared. Death inspires The Fool to consider the major transformation they've gone through since the beginning of their journey, when they were still bright-eyed and even foolish in their innocence. Reflecting on all of the other lessons learned thus far, Death teaches The Fool about transformations and transitions. Beginnings and endings are a natural part of life, and Death simply represents the reflective, transitional periods between the two.

Temperance

The idea of Temperance is next presented to The Fool. Temperance teaches them about balance, along with the importance of seeing all the opportunities and possibilities available in a situation in order to problem-solve effectively. Temperance also warns them about the dangers of overindulgence.

"Engage in everything with careful moderation. Beware of excess," Temperance advises. The Fool struggles a bit with this last lesson and ends up overindulging quite a bit.

The Devil

In the midst of this overindulgence, The Fool finds themselves face-to-face with The Devil. The Devil has a warning for them: "You are letting this excess take over your life. Though you may feel like the situation is out of your control, remember that your life is your own, and you alone have the power to fix this." The Fool smartens up, gets their act together, and walks away from The Devil a wiser and more mindful person.

PHYSICAL SELF-CARE TIP: AVOID THE DEVIL'S TRAP WITH MINDFUL EATING

The Devil is quite the sly archetype, tempting you to overindulge at every turn. Squash their tricks with one of your own: mindful eating. This practice of tuning in to the five senses as you slowly and deliberately enjoy a meal rather than scarfing the food down in front of the TV or while scrolling through social media allows you to avoid eating past the point of being full. It also brings your attention to situations where you may eat for the sake of boredom or other unpleasant emotions, or simply because the food is there.

The Tower

When night then falls on The Fool's Journey, they slumber in a tall, rickety Tower. During a fierce, unexpected storm that night, The Tower is struck by lightning and comes tumbling down. This represents a time of major upheaval, sudden change, and total destruction. The Fool escapes from the disaster unharmed, but this experience inspires them to rethink what's really important in life, recognize the impermanence of everything material, and understand the unpredictability of life.

The Star

The Fool continues along their path that night and eventually rests for a moment beside a lake. The reflection of a bright Star shines on the water, inspiring them to dream about the possibilities of the future. The Star reminds The Fool to have hope.

The Moon

Looking skyward at The Moon, The Fool is then struck by the idea of larger, unseen forces being at play in their life. While considering The Moon, The Fool recalls The Tower that fell and ponders the ideas of illusion and deception. They resolve to continue along the journey with eyes wide open, ready to see things for what they really are.

The Sun

In the morning, The Sun shines brightly, filling The Fool with warmth and happiness. It's a bright new day. With the deep lessons of the night before still fresh in their mind, The Fool is grateful to have survived The Tower collapse and dances in the sunshine. The Sun represents a very happy, positive sort of awakening. It inspires The Fool to appreciate the little things in life, and to celebrate how far they've come.

Judgment

Judgment is met next, with loud fanfare, to teach The Fool about the importance of self-forgiveness. The Fool has made mistakes, yes—but they have learned from them. They have put in so much work along the journey to better themselves. They corrected their negative behavior patterns and toxic, ignorant ideologies, and they are truly worthy of self-forgiveness. The Fool's conscience is cleared, and they move forward with their life, free from encumbering guilt.

The World

After letting go of this guilt, The Fool comes to the final figure of the major arcana: The World. This card signifies the completion of The Fool's fully realized journey. It also represents all the knowledge The Fool has acquired along this adventure. The World says, in a warm, congratulatory tone, "You've done it! You're whole, and you're ready to share what you've learned with others."

The Fool's Journey and You

The Fool's Journey teaches you the lessons everyone needs to learn during their time here on Earth. Whenever a major arcana card comes up during a tarot reading, pay close attention to the lessons it represents. Consider The Fool's Journey and what they learned from each figure they met along their path to enlightenment. When you draw a major arcana card, ask yourself questions like "How can the lesson of this card be applied to my life now? How would the figure represented by this card advise me? What warnings would they have for me?"

. . . .

Mental Self-Care Activity: Seek Life Lessons in the Major Arcana

The major arcana have so many important lessons to teach you. This activity will help you understand how to interpret these messages in your tarot readings.

Items Needed:
- The major arcana cards from 1 tarot deck

Instructions:
1. Shuffle the major arcana.

2. Draw a card.

3. Ponder the meaning of the drawn card, keeping The Fool's Journey in mind. Where are you in your own journey right now? What major theme does this card represent? How can you apply its lessons to your life? Ask yourself these questions and use their answers to help you understand your own path more deeply.

The Basics of Tarot Numerology

Now that you have a better understanding of the major arcana, let's delve into the minor arcana and how to use numerology and the four suits to uncover the many lessons these cards can provide!

To recap, the minor arcana in the standard tarot deck contains fifty-six cards, broken into four suits. These suits—Cups, Wands, Swords, and Pentacles—each contain four court cards and ten numbered cards. Each of the court cards—Page, Knight, Queen, and King—represent personality archetypes (turn to Part 2 to read about each archetype), while each number has a specific meaning (a.k.a. tarot numerology). These meanings can then be applied to each suit. I've broken down the numerology of the cards in a helpful reference chart here:

TABLE OF TAROT NUMEROLOGY	
I	New beginnings, potential
II	Balance, decisions, unions, partnerships
III	Creativity, community, teamwork, collaboration
IV	Solid groundwork, careful manifestation, thorough planning
V	Conflicts, power struggles, friction, changes
VI	Calm states of mind, peaceful communication, harmonious situations
VII	Assessment, the importance of hard work, self-reflection
VIII	Mastery, accomplishment
IX	Wish fulfillment, meeting goals, abundance
X	Completion, reaping rewards, the culmination of knowledge, life cycles

Exploring the Suits

The four tarot suits within the minor arcana each have different element, time, season, and crystal associations that can be used to gain further clarity when interpreting a reading. The elemental suit associations can help you discover which of the four natural elements of the universe (Water, Fire, Earth, Air) you need to connect with in order to balance your energy. For example, maybe you've been feeling scattered lately. Drawing a card under the Earth element is a sign that you need to take some time to ground yourself now. The time and season associations for each suit can also give you a ballpark idea of when an event in your life may take place. For example, maybe you're using a tarot reading to explore when you'll meet a new romantic partner, or when you can expect to move into the next phase of a professional journey. Use the time and season associated with the suit you draw to determine the timeframe of the event interpreted in the reading. The crystals associated with each suit can be used to boost the energy of a tarot reading that involves a card or cards within a drawn suit. You'll learn more about using crystals in Chapter 7.

Each suit also offers a question to ask yourself about your current self-care routines or an aspect of your life that may be in need of more intentional care. You can then use your answer to this question to improve current routines or create new ones.

CUPS

The suit of Cups represents emotions, including love, empathy, and those you get from your gut. It has deep, fluid energy that can be quite tumultuous. Each card in this suit features one or more gilded cups, depending on the numerology of the chosen card.

- **Element:** Water
- **Time Association:** Months
- **Season:** Summer
- **Crystals:** Larimar, amethyst, rose quartz, fluorite, moonstone
- **Self-Care Question:** How can my self-care routines help me remain balanced while I allow myself to feel deep emotions?

WANDS

The suit of Wands represents action, creativity, and passion. It has warm, enthusiastic energy that propels you through challenges and toward whatever goals you're passionate about. Each card in this suit features one or more magical wands, depending on the numerology of the chosen card.

- **Element:** Fire
- **Time Association:** Days
- **Season:** Spring
- **Crystals:** Carnelian, aragonite, sunstone, amber, citrine
- **Self-Care Question:** What sets my heart on fire?

SWORDS

The suit of Swords represents thought, power, clarity, ideas, and challenges. It has swift and intense energy. Each card in this suit features one or more mighty swords, depending on the numerology of the chosen card.

- **Element:** Air
- **Time Association:** Weeks
- **Season:** Autumn
- **Crystals:** Opal, topaz, tiger's eye, turquoise, lapis lazuli
- **Self-Care Question:** How can I slice through mental fog to find clarity in a certain situation?

PENTACLES

The suit of Pentacles represents wealth, careers, the ego, and the physical realm. It has very grounding, stable energy. Each card in this suit features one or more glittering pentacles (or "coins"), depending on the numerology of the chosen card.

- **Element:** Earth
- **Time Association:** Years
- **Season:** Winter
- **Crystals:** Petrified wood, obsidian, onyx, jasper
- **Self-Care Question:** How can I create more stability in my life?

Putting It All Together

Now you can combine your new knowledge of tarot numerology with what you've just learned about the different suits to interpret the tarot cards! For example, maybe you pull III of Wands as your tarot card of the day. You can determine this card's meaning using tarot numerology (cards marked with the numeral III represent community, creativity, and collaboration), combined with the significance of the tarot card's suit, Wands (which represents creativity and enthusiastic action). So, the III of Wands tarot card tells you that today's a day for diving wholeheartedly into creative, collaborative projects. Start that art project you've been talking about! Move forward with those business plans you've been discussing with colleagues. The III of Wands tells you that you're ready to tackle whatever projects you set your mind to—with flair.

With this solid understanding of how a tarot deck is comprised, you will now be able to dive into the next step: discovering tarot spreads!

Chapter 3

Take Up Space: Exploring Tarot Spreads

Tarot spreads refer to the way in which tarot cards are organized when drawn. There is an infinite number of ways to structure the cards in spreads, but certain spreads are especially helpful when working a little self-care into your day. For example, one-card readings are great for quick insights, such as working more emotional self-care into your routine on a certain day. Three-card spreads are perfect for exploring a relationship or situation in more depth. Use these tarot spreads to reveal the true nature of a relationship, clarify the obstacles you are faced with in a given situation, and discover advice on how to resolve conflicts. There are lots of great tarot spreads out there that can help you focus on your unique self-care needs!

In this chapter, you'll explore each of these tarot spreads, starting with the basics and working your way up to those more advanced card draws. You'll also learn a few different techniques for shuffling your deck.

Experimenting with Shuffling Techniques

Despite what tarot "traditionalists" may say, there's no correct or incorrect way to draw or shuffle tarot cards. Some people shuffle a tarot deck the way they shuffle playing cards. Other people like to shuffle them in a more controlled fashion by choosing sections of cards and moving them around within the deck. I visited a tarot reader once who shuffled her deck by spreading all of the cards out on a table and moving them around to mix them up. Experiment! Try different ways of shuffling to decide which way (or ways) feels right for you.

Selecting Your Cards

As far as selecting tarot cards, the same holds true: Use whichever method resonates with you personally! Doing what feels right for you, versus what you think you *should* do, is a simple way to focus on self-care. After all, the cards are here to serve *you*, not the other way around. Some people draw from the top of a deck after shuffling, while other people look for cards that seem to jump out while shuffling (these are often called Jumper cards). Some tarot readers draw cards intuitively from somewhere in the middle of a shuffled deck. The ways in which I shuffle and draw my cards vary based on my mood, and that's okay too! You don't have to decide on one style and stick with it every time.

Keeping It Simple with One-Card Readings

Now that you are familiar with different methods for shuffling and drawing tarot cards, you're ready to learn more about how to lay them out once they've been drawn. The way you lay out the cards is called a "spread." There are many different tarot spreads out there with varying degrees of complexity, and each one has certain unique uses in each of your self-care routines. Many tarot readers pull a single card each morning to give them insight into the themes or lessons they will encounter in the day ahead. They then use this information to help them figure out where they can fit self-care into their daily routine.

I use one-card readings to give me straightforward advice about situations I find myself in or problems I'm facing. For example, if I find that I'm struggling to take time for myself, I ask the tarot cards to help me identify problem behaviors or unnecessary activities that I should let go of in order to better prioritize myself. No matter what questions I ask or what problems I'm having, with the advice from the deck in hand, I can use that information to adopt new self-care practices that restore balance to every aspect of my life.

In the following sections, we'll take a closer look at popular one-card tarot spreads and how you can apply them to your own self-care routines.

MENTAL SELF-CARE TIP: MAKE TAROT PART OF YOUR MORNING ROUTINE

Infusing mornings with magical intent helps to manifest a great day. Consider creating a morning ritual of your own! As you wake up, sit up and take a moment to think about the day ahead. What do you hope to accomplish? How will you make time and space for self-care? Once you have your daily self-care goals in mind, grab your tarot cards and do a reading. Choose whichever spread you think will give you the answers you need to begin the day with self-care front and center in your mind. Once you're done, replace the cards in the tarot box, and get your day started! Remember, your morning routine doesn't need to be elaborate or time-consuming to be spiritually effective. By spending the first few minutes of the day on self-care, you make it a priority in your life, and that's half the battle!

"Yes" or "No" with Tarot

This simple one-card spread is great for answering questions with "yes" or "no" answers. If you're looking for a "yes" or "no" answer from your tarot deck, begin by focusing on your question. Be clear and concise while formulating it (before even picking up the deck), and carry that focus into your shuffle. Draw a card when you intuitively feel like the deck is done being shuffled. Continue focusing on that question as you read the card. Upright cards are typically interpreted as affirmative responses, while reversed cards are usually considered negative answers.

For example, try asking the cards, "Is there an area of my life that I should be focusing a little more self-care in?" Shuffle and draw a card. The card drawn will show you where your current self-care routines might be a little lacking, and how to give those routines a boost. Maybe you draw The Empress in the upright position. This tells you that you should be spending more time connecting with nature and manifesting compassionate energy as self-care.

"YES" OR "NO": SELF-CARE FOR YOUR MIND

Every so often, it's important to check in with yourself and make sure that your current self-care routines are still serving you well. A little guidance from tarot can be so helpful in identifying any changes that might need to be made. Start by meditating for a few moments to unclutter your mind. When you feel ready, shuffle the deck while asking, "Do any of my self-care routines need adjustment?" Draw a card and use its orientation and interpretation (see Part 2) to determine if your self-care practices need tweaking, and, if so, how they can be altered to leave you feeling more deeply fulfilled and nourished. For example, if the IX of Cups is drawn, this is a sure sign that you're right on track with your routines. On the flip side, if a tarot card like The Devil is drawn, make sure to keep your self-care practices balanced by exercising moderation.

Card of the Day

Every morning, I roll out of bed, make myself a strong cup of coffee, pour too much vanilla creamer in it, and sleepily sit down at my desk to pull a tarot card of the day. These popular one-card readings offer themes, lessons, warnings, and advice to keep in mind during the day ahead. For example, maybe you draw Temperance as your card of the day. Moderation is the name of the game with this tarot card, so drawing it tells you that you'll need to direct your self-care practices toward staying grounded and avoiding any temptation to indulge in excess today. Staying balanced and keeping a level head are important parts of self-care that will help you be successful!

CARD OF THE DAY: SELF-CARE FOR YOUR BODY

Are you having trouble deciding whether to focus more on proper nutrition, cardio exercises, strength training, or improving your flexibility today? Use tarot to help you choose what aspect of physical self-care to target today. Ask your tarot deck, "Where should I focus my physical self-care today?" Draw a card. If it's part of the Wands suit, focus on nutrition. If it's a Swords card, get your heart rate up with some cardio. A Pentacles card indicates that you should focus on strength training, and a Cups card tells you to work on exercises like yoga or Pilates to increase your flexibility and balance. If the card drawn is part of the major arcana, work on balancing your overall physical self-care practices rather than putting emphasis on a singular aspect today.

Advice Card

One-card advice readings are similar to "yes" or "no" readings, but they are a little more in-depth; you can ask more open-ended questions when pulling an advice card. Start by sitting down with your tarot deck and thinking about your situation. For example, maybe you are struggling to maintain a positive relationship with a particular friend. You might be arguing with them a lot lately, and your relationship feels a bit strained as a result. So, you'd like advice from the cards on how you can help heal the friendship. After all, self-care isn't *just* about you. Self-care also involves connecting with other people in healthy, meaningful ways and recognizing the value of other perspectives as an important part of this process. Focus on the question while shuffling: "How can I heal the rift between myself and my friend?" Perhaps the IV of Cups is the tarot card that comes forward. This card indicates apathy and a checked-out mentality. As an Advice card in this situation, it's letting you know that you recently may have become a bit unconcerned with what's going on in your friend's life. To help heal the rift, check in with them emotionally. Be present and listen. There may be more going on than meets the eye.

SPIRITUAL SELF-CARE TIP:
DRAW A BONUS CARD

I like to pull two tarot cards every morning: the Advice card and a Theme card (which I actually draw first to discover the overall theme for my day ahead). The Advice card then gives me guidance to keep in mind throughout the day. For example, drawing The Hanged Man as my Theme card would indicate that I may be experiencing a change in perspective throughout the day, so I should stay open-minded and ready to think beyond my own understanding. Then, drawing the III of Cups as my Advice tarot card tells me that I need to make time to celebrate my friendships and enjoy creative collaboration today. So, together, these two tarot cards are encouraging me to keep an open mind, specifically in collaborative or group settings. Being willing to see things from other people's perspectives can lead to personal growth!

ADVICE CARD:
SELF-CARE FOR YOUR SPIRIT

Drawing an Advice card can be so helpful when you're trying to make a complicated decision. Have you been struggling to decide if you should make a career change, or perhaps wondering if it's time to plant roots where you are, or leave and explore the unknown? Tarot can guide you! While shuffling your deck, ask your question clearly. When you feel ready, draw a card. Use its interpretation as advice to help you decide on your next move. For example, if you're wondering whether you should build a life where you are or pack up and move elsewhere, and the VIII of Wands comes forward, it's a clear sign that you should deeply consider leaving. The VIII of Wands is a card that signifies travel, change, and accelerated motion. Embrace the change of pace!

Leveling Up with Three-Card Spreads

Though deceptively simple, three-card tarot readings can really pack a punch; there's a lot of insight and guidance to be gained from pulling just three cards! In the following sections, you'll explore the most popular three-card spreads and learn how to apply these spreads to your self-care routines.

Past, Present, and Future

This is a straightforward tarot spread: Think of a situation or person while shuffling your tarot deck; then, when you feel ready, draw three cards. The first card represents the past, the second card represents the present, and the third represents the future. Remember: The future is variable; cards in the "future" position indicate a future that's possible if things continue on their current trajectory, but there's always a chance that this outcome will change.

This spread can be used to find out where your current self-care practices are taking you, and how well they're serving you. The first card tells you where you have come from in your self-care journey. The center card tells you where you are now, and what your current focus is in your self-care practices. Finally, the tarot card that comes forward in the "future" position indicates what area of your life you'll need to spend more energy on in the future in order to grow and reach your personal goals.

PAST, PRESENT, AND FUTURE: SELF-CARE FOR YOUR BODY

If you've recently started a new fitness regimen, meditation practice, or other form of physical self-care, drawing this spread can show you where you were where you first began ("past" position), where you are in your journey now ("present" position), and where you're currently headed ("future" position). For example, say you've been seeing a therapist for a while, and you're wondering how you've changed during this experience, and how you'll continue to grow through your sessions. If Strength reversed is drawn in the "past" position, this indicates that when you began therapy, you were feeling low and powerless. The King of Swords in the "present" position indicates that you're now in a position of mental clarity. Your judgment has improved, and you're doing great! In the "future" position, The Moon may come forward, showing that you're going to be digging deep in therapy soon. You'll be uncovering hidden truths and looking beneath your surface to explore depths you've been avoiding.

Goal, Obstacle, and Advice

This three-card spread is commonly used during conflicts, or times when you are having trouble meeting a certain goal. The first card drawn represents the goal that you're trying to reach. The second card tells about the challenge or conflict that is blocking your success. The third card offers advice on what to do to solve that problem. Heed the advice of the final card to help you achieve your goal!

For example, say you're having trouble making time for self-care. Draw a tarot card to represent your goal (giving enough time to personal care). Then, draw a card to shed light on what challenges are blocking your success. Finally, draw a third card to give you advice on how to resolve these issues. Maybe III of Swords reversed comes forward in the Goal placement. This card represents emotional healing, so, in this reading, it can be interpreted as saying that the goal is to create time for meaningful self-care. If IX of Swords comes forward in the Obstacle placement, this signifies that anxieties and worries are getting in your way and blocking your progress. And if VIII of Wands is drawn in the Advice placement, it may indicate travel. In this case, it can be interpreted as saying that, in order to create time for deep self-care, you should schedule a vacation out of town.

GOAL, OBSTACLE, AND ADVICE: SELF-CARE FOR YOUR MIND

If you're having trouble keeping up with clutter in your home, a little insight from tarot might be helpful. Use this spread to discover what's getting in the way of keeping a tidy home. The Goal card will show you what your objective should be. The Obstacle card will reveal what's truly blocking your success, and the Advice card will advise you how to overcome this problem and be more orderly and organized going forward.

Option A, Option B, and Advice

When you're faced with making a decision between two choices, use this spread for insights into the true nature of both options. For example, I recently had trouble deciding between starting a new project professionally or moving forward with an existing project on which progress had stalled. I drew one card to represent Option A (starting a new project), and the

Ace of Pentacles reversed was pulled. This tarot card sometimes denotes an unsuccessful financial or professional venture. The second card I drew, representing Option B (continuing with an existing project), was Strength. This card indicates leadership, perseverance, and inner fortitude. The final card, Advice, was The Star, which speaks of hope and renewal. So, this tarot spread told me that starting a new venture wouldn't be as successful as continuing with the project I'd already started.

When it comes to the best self-care practices for you, this simple three-card spread can help you navigate your options.

OPTION A, OPTION B, AND ADVICE: SELF-CARE FOR YOUR BODY

Some days, it can be difficult to decide between letting your body rest, or pushing it with a hard workout. To help you make this decision, envision yourself resting while you shuffle your tarot deck, then draw a card. This card gives you insight into what Option A (a day of relaxation) may provide for you. Next, envision yourself in the middle of a difficult workout while shuffling again, and draw another card. This will show you what Option B (exercising) may mean for you today. The final card drawn, Advice, will help you to decide between the two options.

Person A, Person B, and Their Relationship

This tarot spread is a staple in love life readings, though not limited to them. It can also be used to gain insight into relationship dynamics between coworkers, friends, and family members. With these insights in hand, you'll be able to take the best self-care path for you, whether it means taking a break from social settings to recharge your batteries, cutting out a negative relationship that has been weighing you down, or nurturing a new friendship with someone who supports and motivates you.

To start this reading, focus on a particular person while shuffling, then draw a card for this person. This card represents who they are. Then, focus on a second person, shuffle, and draw another card. This card represents who that second person is. Shuffle once more and draw a third card. This card draws energy from the first two cards in order to show the relationship between the two people those cards represent.

So the next time you get into a disagreement with someone, try using this tarot spread for guidance. Draw a card to represent who you are in the conflict and what sort of energy you're manifesting in response to it. Then, draw another card to represent the other person in the conflict, and what sort of energy they're bringing to the table. The third and final card drawn will represent the overall nature of your current relationship so you can hone in on what needs fixing.

If you would like even more insight into a relationship dynamic, you can also pull a Clarifying card. When the third card tells of certain challenges or obstacles in the relationship, the Clarifying card can offer ways to overcome those challenges.

PERSON A, PERSON B, AND THEIR RELATIONSHIP: SELF-CARE FOR YOUR SPIRIT

Have your recently entered into a new relationship? This tarot spread can be used to show your potential compatibility. Begin by focusing on yourself while shuffling, then draw a card to represent what sort of person you are in this relationship. Then, envision the other person, and draw another card to represent them and what qualities they bring to the relationship. The final card drawn represents the nature of your compatibility with each other. For example, the Knight of Cups drawn in the final position indicates romance, true love, and a knight in shining armor. On the flip side, drawing the III of Swords would indicate that this path may lead to heartbreak and emotional turmoil.

Mastering Top Tarot Spreads

Now that you've explored one- and three-card spreads, you can learn more about the "top" tarot spreads. These are a little more advanced, and they can offer an absolute treasure trove of personal insight and guidance in your self-care journey!

Celtic Cross

The Celtic Cross spread is one of the most popular tarot spreads of all time. It's a great spread to use when you are looking for guidance in a particular situation or goal. For example, maybe you are struggling to find direction in life. The Celtic Cross spread can allow you to focus your energy inward and determine the best way to move forward, giving you a sense of clarity and motivation.

So, if you're struggling with a challenging situation or are looking for insight on how to achieve a goal, take some time for self-care and use the Celtic Cross tarot spread to put your mind at ease. Check it out:

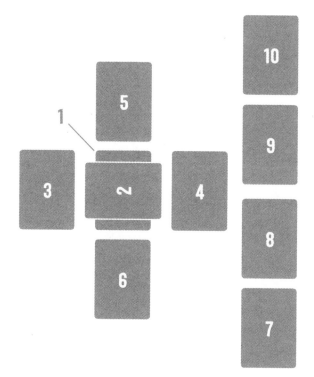

- **Card 1:** The Situation or Goal. This card represents the overall theme of the personal situation or goal on which the reading is based.
- **Card 2:** The Challenge. This card, placed atop the Situation card, gives insight into any major problems or obstacles associated with the theme of the Situation card.

- **Card 3:** The Recent Past. This card tells of the events in the recent past as they relate to the situation or goal at hand.

- **Card 4:** The Near Future. This card tells of related events that may occur in the near future.

- **Card 5:** What's on the Forefront of Your Mind (Above). This card tells you about what elements you are consciously focused on regarding the situation or goal.

- **Card 6:** The Subconscious Mind (Below). This card gives valuable insight into what your true, possibly hidden motives are.

- **Card 7:** Advice. This card offers advice on how to ensure a favorable outcome to the situation or goal, and how to best address the Challenge card.

- **Card 8:** External Influences. This card tells us about external factors influencing the situation that are out of your hands. After all, not everything is within your control.

- **Card 9:** Hopes or Fears. This card represents either your hopes for the situation or goal, or your fears. To determine which of these aspects your drawn card applies to, it should be interpreted intuitively.

- **Card 10:** Outcome or Future. This card gives you an idea of what the future will hold for the situation or goal if things continue along their current trajectory. If you pull an unfavorable card here, don't panic! Take it as a warning: It's time to change things up.

CELTIC CROSS: SELF-CARE FOR YOUR SPIRIT

The Celtic Cross tarot spread can give you a wealth of insight about where you are in life and how to level up to a higher vibration. Begin by centering yourself through meditation, then shuffle the deck and draw a card. This card shows your ideal self. The next card drawn shows the nature of the personal obstacle you need to overcome in order to grow. Cards three and four represent themes in your recent past and immediate future, respectively. The fifth card reveals the area of your life that has most of your current attention, while the sixth card shows you where your focus is subconsciously. The seventh card gives you advice on how to overcome your challenge (card two), and the eighth card pulled reveals what factors in this situation are out of your hands. The ninth card represents either your hopes or worries about reaching your goal (use your intuition to decide which). Finally, the tenth card shows what the future has in store for your journey toward personal growth, provided that things continue on their current trajectory. This spread gives you a lot of information. Take time to contemplate it and let its messages really sink in.

Week Ahead

The Week Ahead tarot spread is another immensely popular spread, and there are countless variations you can try out. The following is the version I use to uncover what lessons and themes I can expect to come into contact with over the next seven days. You can use these themes to decide what kinds of self-care will be most beneficial for you that day or week. For example, if you pull a Sun card for Monday, The Sun themes of success and positive outcomes can be used to practice a self-care activity that takes note of your blessings or celebrates a job well done. Take a look:

- **Card 1:** Sunday. This card shows the overall theme for Sunday.
- **Card 2:** Monday. This card shows the overall theme for Monday.
- **Card 3:** Tuesday. This card shows the overall theme for Tuesday.
- **Card 4:** Wednesday. This card shows the overall theme for Wednesday.
- **Card 5:** Thursday. This card shows the overall theme for Thursday.

- **Card 6:** Friday. This card shows the overall theme for Friday.
- **Card 7:** Saturday. This card shows the overall theme for Saturday.
- **Card 8:** This card shows the overall theme for the entire week.
- **Card 9:** This card gives you advice to keep in mind for the week. When faced with challenges or obstacles, look to your Advice card for guidance.

SPIRITUAL SELF-CARE TIP: TRACK YOUR WEEK AHEAD SPREADS WITH A DAY PLANNER

My day planner is filled not only with appointments and work deadlines but also with the predictions and advice I've drawn from my regular Week Ahead tarot spreads. Every Saturday, I draw this spread, then crack open my planner and scribble a couple of words to keep in mind for each day based on the tarot cards I drew. For example, say The Tower shows up in my Wednesday placement during a Week Ahead spread. The Tower represents instability, major changes, and unexpected upheavals. So, in my day planner, I write the name of the tarot card I drew, The Tower, along with a few words that represent the card: "Expect unexpected changes today. Stay strong!" This helps me keep track of my predictions, gives me advice to keep in mind, and helps me plan out what kinds of self-care practices to work into my schedule throughout the week!

WEEK AHEAD: SELF-CARE FOR YOUR BODY

Use this tarot spread to plan your workouts for the week! Begin by shuffling your tarot deck while envisioning yourself exercising. When you feel ready, begin drawing cards. The first tarot card drawn gives you workout advice for Sunday. Continue drawing cards for each day of the week. Then, pull an additional card to give you insights to keep in mind throughout your week of physical self-care. Cups cards represent days of rest or gentle workouts, like light yoga. Cards of the Wands suit denote days that should be focused on increasing stamina. Pentacles cards show days that you should do strength training workouts, and Swords cards indicate days when you should go all-in and push yourself with intense workouts.

Elemental

This is a very popular tarot spread to use when exploring what lessons the different magical elements can help you learn, and how those lessons can be utilized in intentional self-care. For example, maybe you have pulled Temperance as your Earth card. Since the Earth element is linked to material things, careers, and finances, and since the Temperance card reflects moderation, you know to practice self-care that doesn't overindulge the senses but instead grounds them, like a meditation activity.

When creating the Elemental tarot spread, use a compass to make sure you're facing North, so that the card placements line up with the elemental directions.

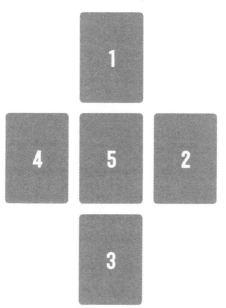

- **Card 1:** Earth (North). What are your financial goals? In which direction is your career headed? This card tells of lessons you need to learn relating to the physical, earthly realm, particularly relating to finances, material possessions, and professions.

- **Card 2:** Air (East). Have you been experiencing writer's block? Maybe you've been feeling as though you're in a fog, or you're having trouble focusing. This card shows you how you can find mental balance and get over any mental blocks you may be experiencing.

- **Card 3:** Fire (South). This card is all about action. What area of your life needs more intentional action from you? Have you been coasting on autopilot in some way? You can use this card's message as inspiration to shake yourself out of a rut and find motivation again.

- **Card 4:** Water (West). This card relates to your relationships and emotional health. How can you stabilize your emotions or current relationships with friends, family members, or a significant other? Use this card to reveal hidden truths about your inner emotional self, and how you can better handle and/or express these emotions.

- **Card 5:** Spirit (Within/Center). What do you need in order to feel fulfilled? This card shows you who you truly are at this period in your life. You can use this knowledge to explore how best to cultivate and maintain balance between mind, body, and spirit.

Spiritual Self-Care Activity: Gain Insight from Elemental Crystals

Each spiritual element has crystals and stones associated with it, such as petrified wood, garden quartz, and hematite for Earth; sodalite and desert rose selenite for Air; carnelian, aragonite, and vanadinite for Fire; amethyst, rainbow fluorite, and enhydros for Water; and indigo gabbro, Tibetan quartz, and celestite for Spirit. Incorporating these crystals into an Elemental tarot spread can help the entire reading vibe higher because crystals enhance the energy of the elements, so you can connect with their messages more deeply. A deeper understanding can then lead to more effective self-care.

Items Needed:

- Crystals or stones associated with each of the five magical elements
- 1 tarot deck

Instructions:

1. Gather your crystals and shuffle your tarot deck while asking, "What lessons do I need to learn from each magical element?"

2. Hold a crystal associated with Earth and meditate with it for a moment, attuning yourself to its energy. As you do this, try bringing to mind the colors associated with the element Earth: brown and green. This will help prevent your mind from straying.

3. Draw a card for the Earth position when you feel ready, and place your crystal atop the card.

4. Repeat steps 2 and 3 for each element. If you feel you need to shuffle again at any point before drawing the next elemental card, do so.

5. When the spread is complete, look at the card you have drawn for each element to see what lessons each drawing can help you learn!

ELEMENTAL: SELF-CARE FOR YOUR SPIRIT

The Elemental tarot spread can be used to identify elemental imbalances in your life and give you tips on how to correct them. For example, perhaps you draw the Ace of Wands reversed (which commonly indicates creative frustration and blocks) in the Fire position. Take this as a sign to reconnect with the Fire element by lighting a candle and meditating on the flame, gazing into or dancing around a bonfire or lit fireplace, or lighting a favorite herb in a fireproof container as an offering to the Fire element. This will restore balance in your life and clear creative blockages.

Making Tarot Spreads Intuitively

Now that the standard tarot spreads have been properly discussed, it's probably time for this disclaimer: I don't always follow these. In fact, most of my readings are done intuitively, without using a set spread.

Gasp! How can this be? Well, I began reading tarot using set spreads, but, as I became more familiar with the cards and the process of reading tarot, standard spreads began to feel confining at times. I wanted to let the cards speak to me in their own way, free from the parameters of a set spread. So, I started letting them deliver messages to me through intuitive readings that let them do the "talking."

Once you have a good grasp of the cards, you can create your own intuitive spreads. To do so, simply shuffle the cards while thinking of a situation, person, or event that you would like to gain more insight into. Then, pull cards until you intuitively feel that the deck is done "speaking." Typically, you will draw anywhere from three to seven cards. Then, interpret the cards you drew by noticing the connections between their meanings—and the connections to the situation, person, or event you created this spread for. Simply put, let the cards tell you their story.

PART 2

SELF-CARE AND THE CARDS

By now you have read about the major and minor arcanas, The Fool's Journey, numerology and minor arcana suits, and popular tarot spreads. So it's time to get down to the nitty-gritty—the meanings of each individual card and what they mean for your self-care. There are upright and reversed position meanings to explore and unique images to take a closer look at. Some people assume that reversed cards are always negative, but this isn't the case! Reversals often provide interpretations that indicate the upright energy of the card is experiencing a blockage or imbalance—interpretations which help you better understand where you can make improvements to your self-care routines and restore balance to your life.

In this part, you will find comprehensive interpretations for each tarot card, beginning with the major arcana. I have also included unique self-care activities for the mind, body, and spirit within each interpretation, so you can easily apply each card's lessons to your personal routines. You will also discover beautiful illustrations—one for each card—that will help you identify cards in your own deck and follow along with the detailed interpretations provided in this part. I've written these sections using a modern, nonbinary lens that still honors the traditional symbolism of each card. Note that court cards and major arcana archetypes can represent people of any gender, which is why I use they/them pronouns when describing them. Traditionally feminine tarot cards such as The Empress can represent someone who is feminine of center, and traditionally masculine cards such as The Emperor can represent someone who is masculine of center—however, this isn't always the case.

Chapter 4

Major Arcana Interpreted

The major arcana are what most people first think of when it comes to the world of tarot. From The Hanged Man and The Lovers to Death and The Empress, these twenty-two magical cards certainly make an impression. But far beyond that, they open the door to layers upon layers of deeper meaning in your life, from personal obstacles to relationships with loved ones—and more.

There is a lot to unpack here, and fortunately this chapter is here to help! The following pages offer an in-depth exploration of each card in the major arcana, beginning with a description of both the traditional illustrations associated with that card, as well as more modern depictions you may see depending on your chosen deck. You'll next move into the upright and reversed interpretations of the card, then discover mental, physical, and spiritual acts of self-care specifically tailored to those insights. Ready to learn more? Let's get started!

The Fool

0

THE FOOL

The Fool tarot card is numbered 0. It may depict a figure resembling a court jester, or a symbol related to the jester. In many popular decks, the figure appears to be on a journey. Sometimes, The Fool is depicted looking skyward, not watching the path ahead. Due to this inattentiveness, The Fool steps out over a cliff.

Interpretation

You, lucky duck, are at the very beginning of an exciting, life-changing journey. You're about to go through a metamorphosis! *Hooray!* This can refer to many different types of exciting adventures. Are you in the planning stages of a big project at work? Maybe you're just starting your self-care journey and are implementing new routines to improve your mental, physical, or spiritual health. Have you recently entered into a new relationship that just feels so *right*? The Fool tarot card can even indicate literal travel!

No matter where you're headed or what you're up to, The Fool is eager (and just a little naïve) as they bravely step out into the great unknown. The Fool trusts that the universe will catch them if they fall, and it will! This card is telling you that the universe has your back. Now this doesn't mean you shouldn't look before you leap. What's the old saying? Oh, yes: "Pray, but row away from rocks." Be sensible. This card tells you to go forth courageously into new adventures, but remember to remain self-aware enough to stay out of any potentially sticky situations.

· ·

Self-Care Card Activities

Mind: Prepare for your "foolhardy" adventure by incorporating some self-care rituals that center your mind. For example, try writing down your goals for the day in a daily planner or journal.

Body: Mornings can be hectic, and many people don't make time to eat a well-balanced breakfast. Try waking up a little earlier than usual and eating a delicious, healthy breakfast to set yourself up for a positive day.

Spirit: To better embrace your own adventure, connect with the element of Fire. Try meditating while watching the flickering flame of a candle, or carry crystals associated with the Fire element, such as carnelian, garnet, or ruby.

· ·

The Fool Reversed

Simply put, The Fool in the reversed position presents itself in a reading when you're being a bit foolish. Have you been making some impulsive, precarious moves in your life lately? Maybe you've been taking unnecessary risks, or reacting hastily in situations that call for more forethought. Over-idealism is also a theme of The Fool card in this orientation. When this card shows up reversed, make sure that you're seeing things as they really are. Beware of the temptation to look through rose-colored glasses. Are you seeing the truth of a situation, or just what you want to see? Be pragmatic now, and be honest with yourself. You don't need to retreat into your shell and be afraid to step foot outside your door, but don't be foolhardy, either. Find your sensible equilibrium. Get organized, and plan ahead to make sure all your actions are deliberate; a little bit of planning now will prevent regrets later.

The Magician

This tarot card is numbered I. Here, The Magician's arm is aimed skyward, wand in hand. In some tarot decks, this image features the full figure of The Magician, with their other arm pointing down to Earth. This signifies the link created by The Magician between the physical and divine realms. Traditionally, the cloak this figure wears is both white, symbolizing a divine connection, and red, marking their connection to Earth. Many decks also feature an infinity symbol floating about The Magician's head like a halo. In traditional decks, there's also a table in front of The Magician, featuring tools that represent the four elements: a cup (Water), a sword (Air), a pentacle (Earth), and a wand (Fire).

Interpretation

This card has such powerful, raw energy to it. It contains the sacred spark of creation. When The Magician is drawn in a reading, it's a sure sign that you absolutely have the power to manifest your goals now. The time is right for new beginnings: You've got the cosmic green light—a precious go-ahead from the stars! Concentrate on your raw potential and work it into something tangible. You have everything you need to create your own sort of magic. There's a divine energy swirling around in your head like a sparkly little whirlwind. Catch a spark, create a plan, and run with it.

. . . .

Self-Care Card Activities

Mind: Your creativity is flowing; this is a great time for major brainstorming sessions, so carry a pocket-sized notebook with you and jot down every idea that comes to mind.

Body: The Magician's whirlwind of activity can sometimes feel overwhelming. Throughout your day, practice deep breathing. This little oxygenating exercise will help you to think more clearly so that you can turn The Magician's inspiring energy into meaningful productivity.

Spirit: It's easy to get swept up in the whirlwind of raw energy surrounding The Magician. Stay grounded by opening and energizing your root chakra. To do this, stand with your head high and back straight. Visualize red, stabilizing energy at the base of your spine (where the root chakra is located).

. . . .

The Magician Reversed

When The Magician comes forward reversed in a tarot reading, it often signifies that you're standing in your own way. Is there an area of your life in which you might be self-sabotaging your own success? Maybe you're just not believing in yourself. Recognize your own talent and potential! You are so capable. Don't let your skills and natural abilities lie latent and unused: Put them to work! Do what you need to do to find your motivation and get that energetic pep back into your step. Work movement into your self-care: Do some stretching or yoga. Go for a walk outside in nature and deeply breathe in fresh air. Gather a few crystals that help promote focus and provide motivation, like vanadinite or aragonite, and keep them on your desk for inspiration.

The High Priestess

II

THE HIGH PRIESTESS

The High Priestess is numbered II. Here depicted with the regal symbol of a crown, many popular decks will portray The High Priestess themselves, stationed between two pillars, one labeled with a "B" and the other with a "J." The former stands for "Boaz," which means "strength," and the latter for "Jachin," which means "he establishes." According to the Christian Bible, these were the two pillars that stood on either side of the Temple of Solomon. A crescent moon is also pictured, representing a connection to the subconscious mind, the great mysteries of life, and lunar magic.

Interpretation

The presence of The High Priestess tarot card is a call to dig deeper. Contemplate your decisions carefully, and be acutely aware of every possible choice available to you. Investigate your options thoroughly now to make informed decisions rooted in logic. This is a time for being real with yourself! This card also indicates that it is a great time for shadow work (see Chapter

8 for more details on the shadow-self); uncover your own problematic behaviors, dig deep, and pull those weeds up by the roots.

· ·

Self-Care Card Activities

Mind: Sound healing will help you delve more deeply into your own consciousness. Bust out your singing bowls, and get into a meditative state. If you don't have singing bowls, you can find audio clips online. Close your eyes, and let the vibration draw your mind inward.

Body: The High Priestess encourages you to be honest about your challenges and to work on yourself. Try out an alternative body treatment like craniosacral therapy to release deeply rooted tension.

Spirit: Make time to carefully think about what's really motivating you. Be honest with yourself about where you are in your journey and where you want to go. What are your goals and intentions? What obstacles stand in your way? Evaluate your plan of action to make sure it's in alignment with your true intentions.

· ·

The High Priestess Reversed

Reversed, The High Priestess indicates that your intuition is calling out to you, but you're not hearing it. Is this by choice? Maybe, deep down, you know the truth of a situation, but you don't feel ready to acknowledge it or deal with it. Whenever you ignore your intuition, its call grows louder and louder and becomes more and more uncomfortable. Sometimes, recognizing harsh truths is unpleasant, and the implications of those truths on your life may be tough to deal with. Nevertheless, it's time to get your head out of the sand. You can't live your whole life pretending not to see things for what they are. You have the power to face the music and handle it.

The Empress

The Empress card is numbered III. Here it features The Empress's crown, along with the Venus symbol of love, sexuality, passion, beauty, inspiration, and relationships. Some decks depict The Empress as being pregnant or plus-size, representing fertility and abundance. The Empress's head crown is often made of twelve stars, representing the twelve months of the Gregorian calendar year.

Interpretation

The Empress is a compassionate, nurturing figure. When this tarot card presents itself, it can be a call to be patient with yourself and to spend time on tender self-care. Don't rush the process. The Empress also speaks of abundance, grace, and beauty. This tarot card sometimes comes forward as a reminder to reconnect mindfully with those qualities. The Empress signifies comfort, luxury, and deep, personal fulfillment. Celebrate where you are in life now, and remember to maintain a loving, compassionate heart.

Self-Care Card Activities

Mind: Go outside in nature. Take note of all the beautiful things you experience: This will help you embrace The Empress's positive, grateful mindset.

Body: Incorporate nature into a physical activity. Take your dog for a walk on a nature trail, call up friends and plan a day of hiking, or rent a kayak for a couple of hours and enjoy the serenity of the water.

Spirit: The Empress is a card of abundance, so now is a great time to remember those who are less fortunate than you are. Make a donation to your local animal shelter, or volunteer to walk a few pups! Donate to a homeless shelter, or help hand out meals at a soup kitchen.

The Empress Reversed

The Empress tarot card sometimes shows up in the reversed position when you're being overly dependent on others. Asking for advice can be a very smart move, but know that ultimately your decisions are yours to make. Don't let the opinions of others drown out your own inner voice. Make time to reconnect with yourself. Stand on your own two feet, and walk tall! The Empress reversed can also indicate that you've been neglecting yourself in some way. Have you been taking care of yourself the way you should? How's your mental health? Are you feeling balanced and capable, or are you leaning on someone (or something) as a crutch? Do what you need to do to restore a degree of independence and equilibrium in your life. Meditate to center yourself, and listen to your inner voice. Trust your gut: You've got this!

The Emperor

The Emperor card is numbered IV. In this depiction, The Emperor is represented with their royal crown, as well as an ankh, the Egyptian symbol for eternal life. In many popular tarot decks, The Emperor is seated on a solid throne featuring rams' heads to symbolize the planet Mars and the astrological sign of Aries, which this card is associated with. Traditionally, The Emperor is seen wearing armor. A vast and majestic mountain range may also lie behind The Emperor, suggesting that this figure is backed by a solid and time-honored foundation.

Interpretation

The Emperor is an authoritative tarot card that presents itself when self-discipline is called for. This card is indicative of a time when listening to the head rather than the heart will lead to the best results. The Emperor symbolizes structure and order; manifesting focused, orderly energy will propel you to reach your goals.

Self-Care Card Activities

Mind: It's difficult to be productive and focused when working in a chaotic, messy environment. Make time to clean up your work space. Tidy your desk, deep-clean your drawers, and organize your paperwork. You will feel so much better!

Body: The Emperor encourages self-discipline and self-improvement. Use this card as inspiration to make a small, healthy change to your diet. Consider hydrating more often, cutting out soda, or asking your doctor for vitamin recommendations to support your overall wellness.

Spirit: Now is a great time to address power struggles in your life with confidence and a level head. Value and respect yourself enough to make sure your needs are being met by loved ones, employers, and anyone else who plays a role in your daily life.

The Emperor Reversed

Have you been feeling unfocused lately? Maybe you've been struggling with something emotionally, and you're overindulging as a coping mechanism. This tarot card in the reversed orientation is a bit of a wake-up call. "Pull yourself together," The Emperor says, when reversed. Sometimes, this position indicates that you may have become too comfortable and are shirking your responsibilities. Acknowledging the ways in which you've become a bit lax isn't always very comfortable or easy, but it's necessary for your personal growth. Don't waste time beating yourself up about it, either; what matters is that you pick yourself back up and get to work. What projects have you been procrastinating on? What have you been avoiding? Tackle these things head-on. Try making a manageable to-do list, and checking tasks off as you accomplish them.

The Hierophant

This card is numbered V. The Hierophant is a wise and religious figure, here represented by a holy text and the two keys to Heaven. Often you may see the full figure of The Hierophant in a tarot deck, wearing white, red, and blue robes. The white robes represent a connection with the divine, the red robes represent wisdom in the material plane, and the blue robes are symbolic of the subconscious mind. Traditionally, this figure stands between two pillars of a religious temple.

Interpretation

The Hierophant is a tarot card that recognizes the importance of hierarchies, structure, tradition, and organized communities. It represents conformity and social belonging. When The Hierophant comes forward during tarot readings, it can indicate that there's a lot of instability in your life right now. Find solid ground through tried-and-true methods; now is not the time to blaze your own path. Often, The Hierophant can also indicate a need for more friendship and fellowship in your life. Have you been feeling unfocused? Listless? Lonely? Do you belong to a spiritual or religious organization, like a coven or church? If so, find solace there. Surround yourself with people with whom you share some sort of strong commonality. The Hierophant is here to remind you that there's strength in community.

· ·

Self-Care Card Activities

Mind: The Hierophant wants you to embrace like-minded people who make you feel a sense of belonging. Join a crafting group, or create a book club. Surrounding yourself with people who support your identity will give you a great confidence boost.

Body: Exercise with others to support your wellness and need for community. Get your heart rate up by starting a running group, joining a volleyball team, or signing up for a spin class.

Spirit: Get together with others who believe what you believe. Whether you visit a church, temple, or coven; attend a spiritual gathering; or sign up for a group meditation session, connecting meaningfully with others will fulfill you now.

· ·

The Hierophant Reversed

Reversed, The Hierophant represents an imbalance of power. Are you dealing with an overbearing authority figure? If not, maybe *you* are being an overbearing authority figure in some way. If you're in a leadership position, take care that you're not getting carried away with your power. It's easy to let it go to your head once in a while! The Hierophant reversed also indicates that now is not the time for a rebellion. Rather, try to restore balance in whatever power struggle you're in by using open, tactful communication. What are your needs? What are your wants? Be aware of the differences between the two so you know which issues you should and shouldn't compromise on. Being clear and concise when communicating with others now will go a long way.

The Lovers

The Lovers card is numbered VI. Here, the unity of this tarot card is represented by two wedding rings linked together. Traditional depictions feature two nude figures standing beneath an angel. The presence of the angel signifies a divine blessing over The Lovers. Essentially, it shows that their union is ordained by the divine. In many popular tarot decks, these Lovers are standing in a lush garden, signifying the abundance and peaceful nature of their union. An erupting volcano in the background symbolizes sexuality, fertility, and the passionate nature of this card.

Interpretation

Ah, The Lovers. This is a card that speaks of beautiful unions, harmonious partnerships, and, yes: love—both romantic and platonic. There's a partnership in your life that's moving along swimmingly, and, boy, does it feel great. However, The Lovers card also indicates that there's some sort of a choice to be made here. Know that there's no going backward from this point. You must decide which way to continue, and then make your move.

Neither choice is "wrong" or "bad"—they're simply different, and it's up to you to decide which path you want to take. Use your head, but don't ignore your heart and intuition. If this card shows up in a reading, I suggest doing a separate Option A, Option B, and Advice card spread to give you more insight and advice. The Advice card will tell you what the universe recommends that you do in this situation, and what you should keep in mind when making a decision.

Self-Care Card Activities

Mind: Practice a little self-love. Give yourself a confidence boost by complimenting yourself in the mirror.

Body: Treat yourself to new pajamas in a luxurious, soft fabric that feels great against your skin.

Spirit: Spread a little love by complimenting a stranger. Making small, positive connections with others can totally improve your mood.

The Lovers Reversed

While upright, The Lovers card indicates that partnerships in your life are harmonious and easy. When reversed, the opposite is true. Something's out of sync here. Maybe once-fiery sparks are starting to fizzle and fade. A choice is to be made; look inside yourself to recognize what's worth working on and holding on to, and what should be let go. Remember, it takes two to tango. Both parties in a partnership have to have the same level of commitment to the same goals, or else the very foundation of the union becomes unstable. Is it time to jump ship, or can things be patched up? Do a Person A, Person B, and Their Relationship card spread to get cosmic advice. The final card has valuable insight for you to keep in mind. Take its message to heart.

This card is numbered VII. The Chariot depicts—no surprise here—a chariot. In many versions, a charioteer will also be featured on this card, wearing armor adorned with crescent moons and symbols of alchemy. The star on the chariot signifies a connection with the divine. The Chariot's success is ordained by a higher power; any charioteer controlling it need only use sheer will and the power of their mind, rather than physical reins. Two sphinxes, one black and one white, may also sit in front of The Chariot.

Interpretation

"Victory!" The Chariot shouts. Success is at hand now. Stay focused! Your goals are attainable and within reach. Don't lose sight of them, because they'll be yours if you persevere. It's time to bolster your forces for one last battle—and this one's for the win. Keep your head held high while you face this grand last stand. You can do it! Go for gold! When The Chariot card comes up in a reading that's searching for a positive or negative answer, The Chariot shouts a resounding, affirmative, "Yes!"

· ·

Self-Care Card Activities

Mind: Focus on confidence-boosting self-care. Dress in a favorite outfit that makes you feel powerful.

Body: Try strength training to get the rush of energy you need to see your projects through to the end.

Spirit: The Chariot indicates that a battle is nearly over. Pause, and consider how far you've come. You're doing so well. Be proud of yourself.

· ·

The Chariot Reversed

Are you feeling a little out of control? Has a loved one become very demanding? Maybe you're dealing with an overbearing boss at work. The Chariot comes up in the reversed position when there are a lot of outside factors influencing a situation. This position indicates a feeling of powerlessness. Try looking at things from a new perspective; instead of adopting a victim mentality by default, look inward. Could it be that your current insecurity is getting in the way of your success? Don't doubt yourself now! You have more power than you think you do. It may seem like things are out of your hands, but The Chariot reversed is here to remind you that you're more capable than you're giving yourself credit for. Now's the time to make your move, communicate directly, and make sure the ball ends up back in your court. Even reversed, The Chariot is a victorious card. You have what you need to see this thing through. Get to it!

Strength

The Strength card is numbered VIII. Here, this card depicts a mighty lion. Traditionally, the Strength card features a figure calmly stroking the lion, symbolizing the trusting connection between them. This connection wasn't forged by fire and might, but through gentleness and loving energy. The figure often wears a white robe, signifying the purity of their intentions. An infinity symbol can also be seen on this card, symbolizing an infinite capacity for strength.

Interpretation

This is a tarot card that speaks not of brute force and bulldozing new pathways but of a gentle, calm, collected sort of strength. The Strength tarot card reminds you that there is power in being tender and soft—in showing compassion, and being loving and kind. In a tarot reading, this card signifies that you may be learning these lessons now. It's important to remember to apply these themes to yourself too. Be patient with yourself.

Self-Care Card Activities

Mind: Create a solution for a little problem that's been bothering you around your home. Maybe you've been dealing with a loose floorboard, broken drawer, or squeaky cabinet hinge. Now's a good time to finally make that trip to the hardware store and fix it!

Body: Focus on core exercises that leave you feeling physically centered and strong.

Spirit: Manifest and center your own strong energy by scheduling a Reiki session.

· ·

Strength Reversed

The Strength card in reverse position indicates the presence of some kind of weakness. Have you been doubting yourself lately? You're probably your own harshest critic. Don't let yourself fall into a habit of negative self-talk! Instead focus on building confidence by cutting out any self-bullying habits.

Strength reversed can also present itself when there are unchecked issues with aggression. Have you been abusing your power in any way? Remember that respecting other people's boundaries is absolutely essential. Be careful to recognize any manipulative behavior patterns you may be exhibiting so you can deal with them properly. There are many healthy ways to express anger and frustration, including playing an instrument, painting, or writing. Turn aggression into something constructive. Book a therapy session, or talk through your anger with a spiritual leader.

The Hermit

This card is numbered IX. The imagery of The Hermit tarot card conveys a sense of solitary discovery. Here, you see a single lantern, with one flame flickering inside. In many variations, this lantern is carried by a lone figure wearing a long hooded cloak. They hold the lantern aloft, showing that they're searching for something. Self-discovery, perhaps; enlightenment. The lantern illuminates only a few steps forward at a time, which shows that the journey The Hermit is on is long. Often The Hermit's step is steadied by a staff in their other hand.

Interpretation

Have you been distracted lately, or constantly on the go? Have you been feeling unfocused, or pulled in many different directions? Do you feel stretched too thin? When The Hermit shows up in a tarot reading, it's a clear sign that you're in need of some time alone. Enjoy your own company! Reflect on your accomplishments, recognize and learn from your missteps, and thoughtfully plan the next moves you have to make to reach your goals.

Many people have busy lives and don't make enough time for themselves. The Hermit is a call to tend to your own needs and re-center your focus so the path ahead becomes clear.

. . . .

Self-Care Card Activities

Mind: Making time for introspection will help you feel more centered. Enjoy your own company; take a bubble bath or organize your thoughts in a journal.

Body: Fill your home with cozy vibes. Bring a pot of water to a boil over high heat, toss in a few cinnamon sticks, and turn the heat down to a low simmer. The scent will create a comforting atmosphere.

Spirit: Indigo gabbro, also known as mystic merlinite, helps you dig deep for productive, introspective self-analysis. Set aside a little time alone to meditate with this crystal.

. . . .

The Hermit Reversed

The Hermit often shows up in the reversed position when you're clammed up inside your own shell. Have you been a bit withdrawn lately? Do you feel a little lonely or isolated? The Hermit reversed is a call to get out of your head, and out of the house. Call up a friend, dress up, and go to brunch. Check in with your family. Now's also a good time to get involved in some kind of community activity, like a volleyball team, crafting circle, or book club. When reversed, The Hermit can also indicate that you're neglecting yourself in some way. Are you struggling with self-care? Use this card as a bit of a wake-up call. If you're struggling, remember that asking for help from friends, family, or professionals isn't a sign of weakness. In fact, it takes strength, and, despite what you may be feeling right now, you have what it takes—and you're worth the effort! Create some positive affirmations, and make a habit of saying them aloud to yourself daily.

The Wheel of Fortune

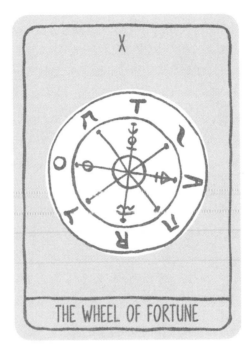

THE WHEEL OF FORTUNE

The Wheel of Fortune is numbered X. This tarot card features the letters "TARO" (for "Tarot"), with the Hebrew letters "YHVH" (for the name of God) between them. The alchemy symbols for sulfur, mercury, water, and salt can also be seen on The Wheel of Fortune, which are the pillars of life in alchemy. In traditional versions, the Greek god Typhon is depicted as a snake beside The Wheel of Fortune, opposite the Egyptian god of the dead, Anubis. An angel, eagle, lion, and bull often appear in the four corners of the card, each bearing wings. These represent the zodiac signs Aquarius, Scorpio, Leo, and Taurus respectively.

Interpretation

The Wheel of Fortune reminds you of the cyclical nature of life. The world is always in motion; time is always moving forward, and nothing in life is ever truly stagnant. So, The Wheel of Fortune is a symbol that change is just around the corner. Who knows what fate has in store for you next? Usually, this card heralds good luck and major life changes. Expect a surprising turn of events, a twist of fate, and the unexpected. If The Wheel of Fortune comes forward during a reading, the answer is a definitive "yes!"

Self-Care Card Activities

Mind: Prepare for whatever changes The Wheel of Fortune heralds by practicing spontaneity. Hop on your bike and just go; enjoy the ride!

Body: The Wheel of Fortune is all about moving energy. Use it as inspiration to get your body moving with a cardio exercise or Pilates class.

Spirit: Now is a great time to make a gratitude list. What connections are you most thankful for in life? Who has supported you and been your cheerleader through it all? What events have shaped you into who you are today? List everything you're thankful for, and reflect with a happy heart on all the ways in which you're fortunate.

. . . .

The Wheel of Fortune Reversed

I'm going to cut right to the chase: The Wheel of Fortune in this position can indicate that bad luck may be on its way. Never fear! Contrary to what you may assume, there are no completely negative cards in tarot. Cards that seem negative can actually be blessings; if you heed their warnings, you can prepare yourself for what's coming, or even avoid a disaster altogether. The Wheel of Fortune reversed is a warning to get moving. Have you been stagnant in some way? Maybe your love life has been rather blah lately? Spice things up! Do whatever you have to do to shake the cobwebs away and wake yourself up. When The Wheel of Fortune shows up reversed during a reading searching for a "yes" or "no" answer, it's definitely a negative answer. In fact, this is a tarot deck's way of absolutely shouting "No!"

Chapter 4 • Major Arcana Interpreted • 73

Justice

The Justice tarot card is numbered XI. Here, it features an image of Justice personified: the scales. In many variations, a figure holds these scales in one hand, while holding a sword in the other. The sword is double-edged, which signifies the duality of every one of your decisions. Two strong pillars may also be seen on either side of this figure.

Interpretation

Justice is a tarot card of rational thought, fairness, and the balance of karma. When Justice is drawn during a tarot reading, it indicates that it's now time to use your head more than your heart. Don't let your emotions get in the way of doing what you know you need to do. Tap into your innate sense of practicality; objectivity is the name of the game here. If you pulled this tarot card while looking for advice, Justice is advising you to take a step back, reflect carefully, and put the whole situation into perspective. Careful reasoning and calm level-headedness is called for. Above all, make sure you're acting in accordance with your moral code. Behave honorably, and be fair in all matters. This will see you through to a successful outcome!

. . . .

Self-Care Card Activities

Mind: Find balance mentally by taking time alone to recharge if you are feeling depleted, or by visiting an art exhibit if you are feeling uninspired. If you're struggling with your mental health, schedule an appointment with a therapist or psychiatrist. Remember: Asking for help when you need it is a sign of bravery, not weakness.

Body: Center your energy and promote balance in your body by making yoga or Pilates a part of your morning routine.

Spirit: Align your energy by honoring Spirit, the fifth magical element. Make sure you're living in honesty and holding yourself accountable for any missteps you take. If you have apologies or amends to make, now is a great time to do so.

. . . .

Justice Reversed

When reversed, Justice indicates a major imbalance in your life. Something's off. Are you being overly emotional when you should be acting more logically? Are you being too cold and detached in a situation that calls for a tenderer, more emotional approach? If you need more insight into this, draw an additional tarot card for clarity.

Justice reversed may also show up in tarot readings when there's legal trouble, or something illegal is going on. If you've been lying, cheating, or acting in other ways that don't align with your moral code, Justice reversed offers a frank warning: "Stop! Restore balance to your life and get things back on track." Actions have consequences, and now may be your time to face the music.

The Hanged Man

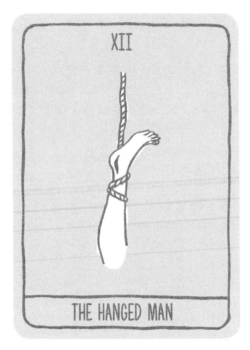

XII

THE HANGED MAN

This card is numbered XII. The Hanged Man tarot card traditionally depicts a figure with rope tied around their ankle. Commonly this figure is hanging upside-down from a tree. In many popular versions, the left knee of this figure is bent, and the left foot is comfortably crossed over the right knee. A halo can often be seen around The Hanged Man's head, symbolizing enlightenment and a high-vibe consciousness.

Interpretation

The Hanged Man card presents itself as a call to see things from new perspectives. After all, things aren't always what they seem to be at first glance. Dig deeper. Be sure to see situations from all sides before taking action.

Sometimes, The Hanged Man tarot card can also be indicative of a major shift in understanding or beliefs. Maybe this epiphany has happened recently, leaving you feeling vulnerable, or maybe it's in the near future. Either way, know that you're growing personally from this experience. Your consciousness and ideas are expanding, and that's a great thing! There's a whole wide world out there. While it's comfortable to stay in your own bubble of perceived safety, stepping out into the unknown will lead to a universe of amazing new experiences. Embrace changes in your consciousness now!

. . . .

Self-Care Card Activities

Mind: Breaking up your daily routines every now and then can help you live more mindfully. Wake up a little earlier than usual and take a scenic route to work. Grab a latte to go, and enjoy the ride.

Body: Exercise your cooking skills by trying out a fun, new recipe.

Spirit: Learn about a religion or spirituality that you're unfamiliar with. You don't have to personally subscribe to any of the beliefs you study; the goal is to broaden your understanding of other perspectives.

. . . .

The Hanged Man Reversed

Reversed, The Hanged Man card can symbolize an imbalance in the way you perceive yourself. Feeling confident is great, but this tarot card often shows up reversed in tarot readings when the ego is overinflated. Put things back into perspective. Your unique views are so valuable, but be sure to recognize the importance and individuality of others too. Don't get so wrapped up in your own greatness that you fail to see the greatness in others.

Sometimes, this tarot card comes forward reversed in a reading when the universe is trying to give you an epiphany but you're closing your eyes to it. Is there a truth in your life you're refusing to see? Often, acknowledging things you would rather not is painful, but know that good will come out of this. After all, burying your head in the sand won't make the truth go away.

Death

XIII

DEATH

This tarot card is numbered XIII. Here, Death is depicted as the classic skull and crossbones. Many variations will give this skull a full skeleton, wearing dark armor. This skeleton is often riding a white horse and carrying a flag. Traditional imagery also features a royal figure who has died. Additional figures may plead with the skeletal Death to spare this figure's life, but Death continues on dutifully.

Interpretation

This is such a commonly misunderstood card! Death heralds transformations, transitions, and metamorphosis; Death is the caterpillar turning into a beautiful butterfly. Changes can be uncomfortable sometimes, sure, but they can also lead to bigger and better things. When Death shows up in a tarot reading, expect major shifts in your life. You could be moving, going through a major breakup, starting up a business, or changing careers. Embrace the change, and know that the future holds beautiful things for you.

Self-Care Card Activities

Mind: Sort through your wardrobe and donate any unwanted clothing to a shelter. It will be easier to keep your closet tidy without all those extra clothes, and you can rest peacefully knowing you've given to people in need—win-win!

Body: Do you get wellness checkups as often as you should? If you've been putting off an appointment, now is the time to make the call and schedule it.

Spirit: Elestial quartz is a crystal that helps you through major transformations and transitions. Wear elestial quartz on a necklace, or carry it in your pocket.

Death Reversed

When reversed, the Death card can indicate that you're feeling trapped, or refusing to move on from something. You should be progressing into the next phase of your life, but the path forward is being blocked by something. Usually, Death reversed indicates that this blockage is something internal rather than external. Are you feeling set in your ways? Have you been hesitant to embrace changes? Have you been feeling stagnant at work? Remember that change can be a great thing—even beautiful. Embrace the unknown now. As self-care, make a playlist of music that makes you feel bold, and dare yourself to embrace the transitions you've been afraid of.

In relationship readings, Death reversed often shows that things should have ended, but you're unwilling to move on. And when Death reversed is drawn in a career reading, give some thought to shaking things up at work. Consider making a big professional shift.

Temperance

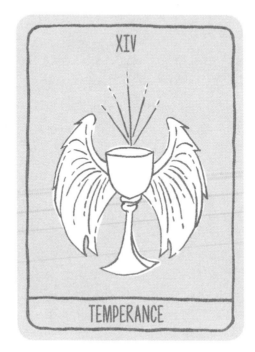

The Temperance card is numbered XIV. Huge, magnificent wings are featured on this tarot card, along with a glistening chalice. In many popular versions, the wings are attached to an angel. This angel often wears a light blue robe and stands with one foot on a stone along the path of life, while the other foot is planted in a flowing river.

Interpretation

The Temperance card teaches you the importance and beauty of balance and moderation. "Be sensible," Temperance says. "Stay centered and level-headed." Think very carefully through any decisions presented to you now. Be sure that you're aware of all the factors involved before you make your choice. Take time to create thorough pro and con lists to help you visually understand and organize your options, if necessary.

When Temperance shows up in a tarot reading, it's often a call to restore balance to your life. Have you been working a lot lately, and not making enough time for family? Maybe you've been pulled in a dozen directions, and your energy has become a bit scattered and unfocused. Be conscientious of how you're spending your time, and make sure to create time to recharge yourself.

· ·

Self-Care Card Activities

Mind: Social media is amazing, but it's important to stay critical of your experience using it. Regularly edit the lists of people you follow. Remove any accounts that don't inspire, entertain, or educate you.

Body: Reflect on your diet and make sure it's well-balanced. Try tracking your eating habits in a journal for a week, then analyzing them to see if any adjustments need to be made to support your wellness.

Spirit: Practice mindfulness through emotional balance. Find healthy ways to express yourself: Journal, paint, or change up your wardrobe.

· ·

Temperance Reversed

When reversed, Temperance warns of the potential dangers of overindulgence. Do a bit of introspective meditation and ask yourself, "Do I feel an imbalance in my life?" Be honest with yourself, and do whatever you need to do in order to restore balance. This position may indicate that you're running away from the daily details of life. Maybe you're neglecting to pay necessary attention to the mundane, but nevertheless very important, aspects of existence. Make a list of tasks you need to complete, and check them off as you go. Be sure to pay your bills, do your chores, and avoid excess now. Life isn't always fun and games, and that's okay! You have everything you need to succeed now. Take care not to throw it all away because you would rather not deal with the particulars.

The Devil

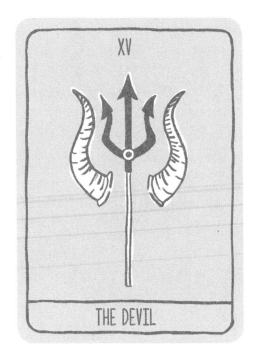

This card is numbered XV. Here, The Devil's horns and trident are shown. Traditional tarot imagery depicts the entire horned image of Baphomet, a mythical creature who is half man and half goat. This creature commonly has bat wings, and its right hand is often raised in a traditional Jewish blessing while its other hand holds a lit torch. An inverted pentagram can commonly be seen above Baphomet's head.

Interpretation

The Devil tarot card presents itself when there's recently been a period of overindulgence. This overindulgence may even have evolved into an addiction. While this can be a frightening card to get in a tarot reading, it's important to recognize that you have the power to free yourself from the archetypal Devil's grasp. The Devil tarot card is a warning that says "Get it together! Restore balance to your life. Don't succumb to your vices; you're stronger than they are." Believe in your own strength, and don't be afraid to seek professional help if this issue is too much to face on your own. Therapists, counselors, support groups, and addiction specialists are great resources. Remember, there's no shame in asking for help. In fact, admitting that you need it is courageous, and a powerful first step.

Self-Care Card Activities

Mind: Make sure you're not getting too wrapped up in your own mind now. Get outside of your head by calling up friends for a brunch date.

Body: Supporting your physical wellness is so important, but it's easy to become obsessive about health and your physical appearance. Examine any negative behaviors or patterns; make sure you're not going overboard or becoming obsessive about your diet or weight.

Spirit: This is a great time for shadow work. Spend time educating yourself on social issues to unlearn toxic conditioning and prejudices. How diverse is your social media feed? Spend time searching for and following a wider range of accounts (the disabled, people of color, etc.) to broaden your understanding of the world.

The Devil Reversed

Reversed, The Devil card shows that you've done it! You've broken free from the grasp of something intense, like a vice, addiction, bad situation, or toxic person. *Congratulations!* You've come out on the other side a stronger and wiser person. Stay the course now. There's temptation to fall back to that vice or toxic situation or person from which you've just freed yourself. This card reversed emphatically says "Don't!" Continue on your current course, and keep a sensible head about you. Remember why you changed a problematic behavior, or left a toxic situation or person behind. Stay focused and keep your goals in mind.

The Tower

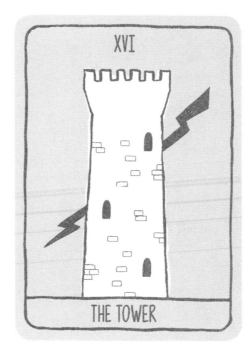

The traditional imagery for The Tower depicts a tall stone tower being struck by a bolt of lightning. In many popular tarot versions, people are seen flinging themselves from the windows of The Tower as it crumbles. A crown can often be seen being knocked from The Tower as well.

Interpretation

Total destruction, unexpected collapse, and chaos are represented by The Tower. In The Fool's Journey, The Tower beneath which The Fool is sleeping is suddenly struck by lightning and collapses.

As The Fool survives this traumatic event, so too can you get through this tough period in your life. Sometimes, things have to come crashing down to pave the way for bigger and better things. While this period may feel chaotic, know that it won't last forever. Do what you have to do to get by now, and worry about the details later. Brighter days are ahead!

Self-Care Card Activities

Mind: Be sure you're making time to check in with yourself regularly. Do a tarot spread reading to access your subconscious and acknowledge your personal truth.

Body: Relax tense muscles by using a crystal facial roller. Pro tip: Store the roller in your refrigerator when not in use for a cooling, ultra-refreshing experience.

Spirit: Focus on energizing your root chakra using crystal healing, a meditation exercise, or singing bowls. Boosting your root chakra can help give you the strength to learn lessons associated with The Tower and get through this rough patch.

The Tower Reversed

Something major in your life has collapsed, but you're refusing to let go of the broken pieces. Maybe a relationship with a loved one is crumbling, or a set of personal beliefs isn't serving you well anymore. No matter what The Tower reversed is specifically referring to in your own life, you're not moving on like you should be. You're digging in your heels when you're supposed to be walking away. Be sure you're seeing things as they really are now. Keep your rose-colored glasses tucked safely away in a drawer. Maintain a cool, practical mindset, hold your head high, and manifest the courage to move on from things and people that aren't in alignment with your spirit. Resisting change will only prolong the grieving process.

The Star

This card is numbered XVII. The Star tarot card features one large, bright star, surrounded by smaller stars. Below the stars sits a pitcher of water. In many traditional versions, this water is divided into two bowls, held by a nude figure. One bowl of water is being spilled onto the lush earth around the figure, while the other bowl is being spilled back into a natural spring.

Interpretation

Have you been through a rough period in life recently? Maybe it's left you feeling a little tired and dazed. The Star speaks of hope and deep rejuvenation. When drawn in tarot readings, this card reminds you to hold tightly to your ideals and find comfort in them. The possibilities ahead seem absolutely endless. Let yourself imagine all of them through a hopeful lens. If you've recently had a major shift in your life, The Star is reminding you to have faith that better, brighter days are ahead. After all, the universe works in amazing, magical ways that you don't always understand immediately. The Star card is a sign to trust that the universe knows what it's doing. Everything will work out for the best! Keep going, keep dreaming, and keep believing.

. . . .

Self-Care Card Activities

Mind: De-stress by avoiding busy, bustling environments that can overwhelm your senses. Instead of going to a loud, wild concert, visit an art museum.

Body: The Star calls for rest. Have a movie marathon at home, and give yourself permission to relax. Pop a bowl of popcorn, invite friends if you'd like, and put on a favorite film series.

Spirit: Invite loving, happy feelings into your life with rose quartz. Meditate with this crystal, or carry it in your pocket.

. . . .

The Star Reversed

Have you been working very hard toward a goal but not seeing the results or progress you expected? Reversed, The Star indicates feelings of loneliness, hopelessness, and a lack of fulfillment. Your unmet expectations have left you feeling bummed out, unappreciated, and even a bit isolated.

Don't meet this energy with frivolous distractions. Now is the time for deep reflection. Take stock of your life as objectively as possible. Where can you take meaningful, productive steps to make things better? Reversed, The Star alludes to an element of denial. Maybe you do know how to improve a situation in your life, but you've been avoiding taking action for one reason or another. The Star reversed is a sign that you need to be brave. Face your truth, own it, and deal with it. Your whole life will be better for it! Ignoring or hiding from the truth of a situation is exhausting. Put that energy to better use by getting everything out in the open, where it can be dealt with.

The Moon

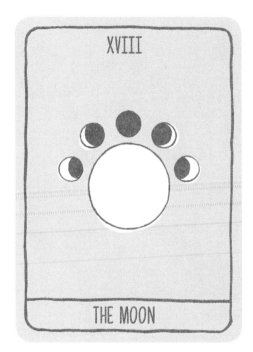

This card is numbered XVIII. Represented in this version by the lunar cycle—the full moon taking center stage—many traditional depictions of The Moon card feature the images of a dog and a wolf howling at the full moon. The wolf represents the untamed shadow-self, and the dog represents the cultivated, tamed self. Two towers can often be seen on either side of these canines, marking the path to enlightenment that lies between them. Popular tarot versions also include a flowing river running in front of the howling dog and wolf, with a crayfish crawling out of its depths.

Interpretation

When The Moon card is drawn in a tarot reading, it signifies that you're feeling helpless, anxious, or worried. Things seem like they're out of your control. And maybe they are—still, The Moon card calls for you to put things into perspective. You could be letting your worry run away with you where things aren't so hopeless or difficult to fix. Be sure that you're seeing situations as they really are.

The Moon also shows up in readings when someone is deceiving you. Pull the wool from your own eyes; make sure you're not letting anyone close to you get the better of you, and beware of manipulation. Look out for yourself, and don't let anyone dull your shine! When The Moon shows up in a tarot reading, it indicates that now is the time to be discerning. Things aren't always as they appear to be at first glance. Remember that if something seems too good to be true, it very well may be. Search for the truth, and use your logic.

· ·

Self-Care Card Activities

Mind: Consider big decisions carefully. Don't make any large purchases until you've thought them through completely, or sign any contracts without thoroughly reading and understanding all of the terms.

Body: The Moon has very serious energy. Lighten it up by laughing. Watch a funny video clip, read your favorite comic, or listen to a hilarious new podcast.

Spirit: Make sure that the people in your inner circle have positive energy and intent. Ask yourself, "Do they have my best interest at heart? Do I feel good when I'm around them?" If the answers are "no," limit your time spent with them, or consider moving on completely.

· ·

The Moon Reversed

Reversed, The Moon often indicates excessive worry, sometimes even to the point of mental illness. Have you been feeling a bit paranoid? Has your anxiety become overwhelming? Maybe you're experiencing a mental imbalance that's coloring your perception of the world. As self-care, manage your mental health now. I take care of my own mental health by seeing a psychiatrist, going to therapy, and incorporating lots of new age healing practices into my self-care routines. Check in with yourself; go for a walk in nature and breathe deeply, meditate, or book a healing session with a Reiki master. Above all, don't be shy about making an appointment with a healthcare professional if things feel like too much to handle on your own. Life gets stressful, and balancing your mental health is absolutely crucial self-care.

The Sun

This tarot card is numbered XIX. The imagery depicted on The Sun card is of a massive, vitalized sun—its rays reaching out toward every side and corner of the card. Traditionally, this sun features warm colors and the addition of a happy young child riding a large white horse beneath it. Four flowers can typically be seen blooming over a tall brick wall behind the child. The child traditionally carries an oversized red flag in one hand.

Interpretation

Cheers, my dear! The Sun indicates that things are bright and lovely now. Bask in The Sun's warm glow; soak up its good vibes, and enjoy the present moment! When The Sun card is drawn in a tarot reading, it usually signifies that a period of hardship is ending. You're finally experiencing a break-through: The storm is over, rain clouds are clearing, and The Sun is coming out in your life. This is a tarot card that calls for celebration. Embrace it!

Self-Care Card Activities

Mind: The Sun demands a big bash. Now is a great time to call up your friends for an impromptu dinner party! No special occasion is needed: Just get together with your nearest and dearest for the sake of it, and have tons of fun.

Body: Try acupuncture. This unique form of physical therapy is great for releasing tension, easing aches and pains, and so much more. You'll walk away feeling energized and ready for some fun! Talk to a professional about how acupuncture can support your own personal wellness, and schedule a session.

Spirit: Spread The Sun's warmth around by sharing your gratitude for all the universe—and the people in it—has given you. Tell a loved one how grateful you are to have them in your life in a heartfelt, handwritten note, or say a little prayer of thanks for your blessings.

The Sun Reversed

The energy of The Sun is still present when the tarot card is reversed, but something is blocking its warmth and light. This reversed position can show up in a tarot reading during a period of sadness or even depression. The Sun's beautiful rays are all around you, but you can't see their shine.

In order to unblock The Sun's light, you need to restore your sense of childlike bliss and wonder. Make time for fun activities that make you happy—no matter how silly they may seem. Paint messily with your fingers. Read a favorite childhood book that has a happy ending. Listen to upbeat music that pumps you up, and dance around your home. Your pets might give you strange looks, but your heart will be overflowing! Also remember that if sadness or depression is too much for you to manage on your own, there's no shame in seeking professional help. Do what you need to do to get your mental health back on track! You deserve to bask in the sunlight.

Judgment

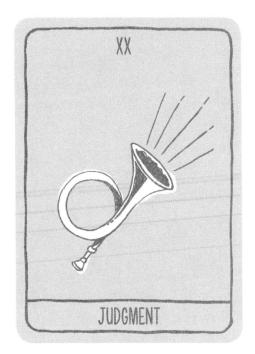

This tarot card is numbered XX. The nature of the imagery featured on the Judgment card is rather biblical: It features the archangel Gabriel's trumpet sounding out. The messenger of God, Gabriel uses this trumpet to raise the dead for Judgment Day. In many traditional versions of this tarot card, you can see the images of people rising from their graves, arms raised and faces skyward. A mountain range can often be seen in the background. The full image of Gabriel is also typically featured in popular tarot decks, donning white robes and blowing into the trumpet.

Interpretation

Like the instrument it features, the Judgment card toots a loud message. It says "Forgive yourself." You've made mistakes, yes, but you're learning from them. Look at how far you've come in life. You're not the person you used to be, and your beautiful metamorphosis is inspiring. Don't waste time on beating yourself up for any missteps you may have taken along your journey. After all, everyone makes mistakes. What matters is that you grow from them—and as the Judgment card is here to remind you, you have. Life is hard, so give yourself some credit and recognize your triumphs! You're doing great.

. . . .

Self-Care Card Activities

Mind: Set yourself up for positivity by making a list of genuine, positive affirmations that resonate with you. Keep it on your bedside table (you can even frame it) so that it's the first thing you see when you wake up each morning.

Body: Have you been lax in your physical self-care routines lately? It's okay: Everyone gets into slumps now and again! Now's a great time to get back into your fitness routines. Go to the gym, take a long walk, or meet up with your old running group.

Spirit: Reconnect with your spirituality. Meditate with crystals that support your third eye and crown chakras, such as amethyst, celestite, and spirit quartz. Make time to commune with whatever higher power(s) you honor.

. . . .

Judgment Reversed

When reversed, the Judgment card indicates that you may be stuck in a negative mental space. You're not letting yourself move on or evolve. For example, do you have a negative behavior pattern you need to work on? Are you holding on to some kind of toxic ideology that needs a revamp? Ask yourself these questions, and be honest in your responses. If an old way of doing things isn't serving you anymore, don't be afraid of change. After all, change can be beautiful, even if it's scary at first. The Judgment card is here to tell you that you have a metamorphosis to go through; let it happen, and you'll come out on the other side as a beautiful butterfly.

Sometimes, Judgment reversed can also indicate that you're being really hard on yourself. You may be self-deprecating or overly critical of yourself. When Judgment shows up in reverse during a reading, I suggest drawing an additional card for advice. This card will show you what you need to do to restore balance to your inner world. You're sure to feel better when you've tended to your inner garden and pulled up any weeds (negativity) growing in your heart.

The World

This tarot card is numbered XXI. Here depicted as the vast Earth we call home, you may also find many traditional versions that feature a person dancing within a laurel wreath. In these traditional versions, you will also see four creatures in each of the four corners of the tarot card, representing the four fixed signs of the zodiac: Taurus, Leo, Scorpio, and Aquarius. They can also represent the four elements: Earth, Fire, Water, and Air. Additionally, the dancing figure in the center of many popular versions typically holds two wands, similar to the one in The Magician card.

Interpretation

The World card drawn in a tarot reading shows you that things are falling into place beautifully now. A long journey or time-consuming project is being completed—*hooray*! You've learned so much along the way; you've come through trials and tribulations, and can now turn the page and begin the next chapter of your life. You've reached a place of cultivated knowledge and maturity, and now is the time to share that story of personal growth with others. The World card in a reading indicates that you should tell the tales of your experiences, so that other people can learn from what you've been through. You're in a coveted place of strength and self-reliance, after all, and you have the power to help others get there too.

Self-Care Card Activities

Mind: Stop any negative self-talk in its tracks and start accepting compliments from others—and yourself—graciously. You deserve them.

Body: Celebrate the joyous messages of The World by dancing! Move and groove to some sweet, sweet tunes. Whether you go dancing with friends at a club or do it in the privacy of your own living room, dancing is good for your body and can put you in a great mood.

Spirit: You've worked hard to cultivate yourself, and it shows. Write an essay about your journey and the valuable lessons it has taught you, and submit it to an online publication or magazine. Share your insights with the world!

The World Reversed

Reversed, The World card indicates that you're not feeling fulfilled. Maybe a project in your life should have been completed by now, but it's ongoing and becoming tedious. The World reversed says "Be patient." Sometimes, plans take a little more time to come to fruition than you expect, and that's okay. Roll with it! Be flexible. Don't lose your motivation just because of a few setbacks.

Sometimes The World card also reveals itself in a tarot reading when you're isolating yourself. Have you checked in with friends or family lately? As self-care, call up some friends and make a date for your local museum. Attend a concert. Try a hot new restaurant. Whatever you decide to do, enjoy this revitalized sense of community. "Don't hide away now," The World reversed says. "Be courageous, and live your life boldly."

Chapter 5

Minor Arcana Interpreted

Pentacles, Wands, Swords, Cups...there certainly is a lot going on within the fifty-six cards of the minor arcana. As you learned previously, the minor arcana is made up of four suits that focus on day-to-day insights. Like the major arcana cards, these can be interpreted in both upright and reversed positions—each lending important and unique details to your reading.

The following pages will bring you on a more in-depth tour of each card in the minor arcana, from upright and reversed interpretations to mental, physical, and spiritual acts of self-care specifically tailored to that card. You will also discover an illustration of each minor arcana card, but keep in mind that designs may vary slightly depending on your chosen deck. So without further delay, let's dive in!

Ace of Cups

ACE OF CUPS

Interpretation

This tarot card is numbered I. The Ace of Cups can often be a sign that new love is entering your life. Whether this love is platonic or romantic, the Ace of Cups indicates you're experiencing a very intense abundance of positive feelings. Many times, this card presents itself when you're so overcome with warm, fuzzy emotions that you're essentially overflowing with them! The Ace of Cups reminds you to allow yourself to feel everything; embrace your emotions now.

Self-Care Card Activities

Mind: Turn your bedroom into a comfortable oasis by splurging on quality bedding and adding lots of cozy throw pillows.

Body: Connect with the emotional Water element by swimming in a natural body of water.

Spirit: Step outside of your usual routines for a cathartic exercise in abstract painting. Expressing your feelings through art is good for the soul.

Ace of Cups Reversed

The reversed orientation of this card can indicate that you're letting your emotions get the best of you. You may be feeling overly emotional and losing sight of the reality of a situation. It's okay: deep breaths! Now is a good time to take a step back and try to look at life through a more practical lens. On the flip side, beware of bottling up your feelings. Don't hide from them: You're allowed to feel! You just have to be careful to express those feelings in healthy ways. As self-care, take some time alone to find your healthy emotional equilibrium again. Meditating with grounding crystals like smoky quartz or black tourmaline can help you restore emotional balance.

II of Cups

II OF CUPS

Interpretation

Get ready to partner up, buttercup! The II of Cups card heralds harmonious unions of all kinds, from professional, to romantic, to friendly. Maybe you've recently made a new friend, or perhaps a new love interest is waiting for you just around the corner. And if you're already in a relationship, you're sailing in sweet, smooth waters. In fact, when this card shows up in a relationship reading, it indicates great compatibility! II of Cups can also be a sign that a major relationship in your life has what it takes to last.

Self-Care Card Activities

Mind: Memorize and recite a love poem! Shakespeare's sonnets are a great place to start.

Body: Harmonious relationships start with your relationship with yourself; set aside a few minutes each morning and night to hydrate your skin with coconut oil or your favorite moisturizer.

Spirit: Strengthen the connection between your conscious and subconscious through a guided meditation.

II of Cups Reversed

When reversed, the II of Cups tarot card speaks of a partnership or romantic union that is not at all harmonious. Is there a partnership in your life that's been traveling on a bumpy road lately? Maybe things aren't going smoothly in a romantic relationship, or you and a bestie have been fighting lately. Follow this reading by asking the deck for advice on what to do about a tumultuous partnership. Formulate your question, shuffle the deck, and pull an Advice card. This final card will give you further insight.

≋ III of Cups ≋

Interpretation

Time to party! III of Cups calls on you to get together with loved ones and celebrate your successes. Have you just finished a project you worked really hard on? Are you beginning an exciting new collaborative endeavor? III of Cups reminds you to take note of your accomplishments and enjoy the fruits of all your hard work. III of Cups can also refer to common celebrations, such as birthdays or holiday parties, or life milestones, such as having a baby, adopting a pet, or buying a house. It's a card of community, friendship, and collaboration. So go out and share these sunny, happy vibes with everyone you love!

Self-Care Card Activities

Mind: This is the time to get together with your best friends! Plan a fun weekend getaway to create beautiful memories that will last forever.

Body: Use a body scrub to exfoliate your skin, and visualize negativity washing off of you as you scrub.

Spirit: Practice speaking to yourself like you would speak to a best friend: with kindness, empathy, and compliments.

III of Cups Reversed

Reversed, the III of Cups card is drawn when you're keenly aware of an imbalance in a relationship. Do you feel like you're doing all of the work on a project? Are your needs not being met by a romantic partner? Speak up! This isn't the time for passive aggression; clearly communicate your needs and perspectives. III of Cups reversed reminds you how important it is to stand up for yourself as self-care. Find your voice and demand fairness!

IV of Cups

IV OF CUPS

Interpretation

Have you been feeling a bit bored lately? Exhausted, even? Drawing the IV of Cups tarot card in a reading can be a sign that life has been feeling heavier than usual. Maybe you've even been a little more wrapped up in yourself than usual lately. The IV of Cups can indicate that you've been dealing with the doldrums by becoming a little self-absorbed, or simply mentally checking out entirely and becoming too apathetic to the world around you. Don't give up now! Shake the cobwebs from your eyes and do what you need to do to stoke your fires. IV of Cups indicates that now's the time to make your move, and get back at it. Life is waiting for you!

Self-Care Card Activities

Mind: Rearrange your furniture for a refreshing change of both scenery and perspective.

Body: Reenergize yourself by doing a cardio workout.

Spirit: Carnelian, vanadinite, and citrine are crystals that can help motivate you and get you back on track. Display them in your workspace to give you the boost you need to get the job done.

IV of Cups Reversed

When reversed, the IV of Cups indicates that you're feeling replenished and rejuvenated. The world really is your oyster—and this is an amazing, coveted place to be in. Have you recently come into a leadership role? If so, remember to consider the opinions and feelings of others while up in that high tower. You've proven that your way works, but others' perspectives have value too. Be sure to maintain your compassionate spirit as you blaze ahead.

V of Cups

Interpretation

The V of Cups shows up in readings when you've recently experienced a setback or loss. Have plans recently gone awry? Are you going through a breakup? No matter what's going on in your life, the V of Cups indicates that now's a great time to take stock of what you *do* have going for you. Also remember that every misstep is a learning opportunity.

The V of Cups also signifies that you may be too wrapped up in your own emotions right now, or even throwing yourself a bit of a pity party. Know that things aren't as hopeless as they seem; rest assured that this feeling will pass. Allow yourself to be sad for a little while if you need to, but don't let regret or disappointment consume you. There are brighter days straight ahead!

Self-Care Card Activities

Mind: Burn a citrus-scented candle or diffuse citrus essential oils. The energizing scent will give you that little boost you need to be productive today.

Body: Work with your hands. Spend some time gardening or doing yard work if the weather permits.

Spirit: Meditate on your blessings. Remember the V of Cups's message: The sun will come out tomorrow!

V of Cups Reversed

V of Cups reversed has one major piece of advice for you: "Let yourself feel." Bottling up feelings only leads to energy blockages, and the effects of energy blockages can manifest in your life in all sorts of negative ways. Acknowledge your feelings as valid, and work through them constructively so that you can move forward. Emotions aren't weaknesses, and there's so much strength in being honest with yourself.

VI of Cups

Interpretation

The VI of Cups is a card of familiarity and innocence. Have you been feeling a little jaded? Perhaps you've seen the harsh side of the world lately, and it's left you a bit bitter. If so, this card is reminding you that there's beauty and goodness everywhere too. You just need to open your eyes to it. Challenge yourself to step out of your comfort zone; you'll have the time of your life while experiencing something brand new, which will help you put things back into perspective. VI of Cups essentially says "Don't let the world turn you hard. Life is miraculous. Enjoy it!"

Self-Care Card Activities

Mind: Reconnect with your sense of wonder and amazement. Visit the ocean and contemplate its enormous depth. Go stargazing. Do something that reminds you that the universe is unimaginably magnificent.

Body: Book a massage session, or make time to massage your own body at home. You'll feel so rejuvenated.

Spirit: Look within to explore what it is that you want, then practice asking for it clearly and effectively.

VI of Cups Reversed

Thinking about the past can be beneficial if you do so through a productive, analytical lens. However, the VI of Cups comes forward reversed in a tarot reading when you're simply not moving on as you should be. Don't let life pass you by while you're busy looking backward—there are so many beautiful things ahead! Focus on self-care practices that pull you into the present moment, like a fun physical activity.

Interpretation

When the VII of Cups comes forward in a reading, make sure you're seeing things for what they really are. Being an idealist is a beautiful thing, but take care not to get so swept up in your fantasies that your perception of reality gets skewed. VII of Cups advises you to keep your feet on the ground; make sure that your decisions are based on solid facts rather than on dreamy illusions.

Self-Care Card Activities

Mind: Staying on top of chores can be difficult: It seems like there's always something to be done! Create a weekly chore chart to help you organize and keep track of these tasks.

Body: Now's the time to do a fun activity to reconnect with the present moment. Get a group of friends together and do something unexpected and physically invigorating, like going on a day-long hike.

Spirit: Ground yourself with a boost of earth energy. Walk barefoot outside in nature, or carry stones that are associated with the Earth element, such as smoky quartz or hematite.

VII of Cups Reversed

While the VII of Cups upright indicates that you're getting too caught up in fantasies, its reversed orientation can allude to distracted, frantic energy. Have you been stuck in unproductive busywork lately? Have you felt as though you're chasing the proverbial carrot on a stick—getting nowhere? The VII of Cups reversed asks you to make time to check in with yourself. Center your energy by meditating with garnet, which aides in cultivating a clear, focused, present state of mind. Rethink your current strategies if you find they're not serving you well.

VIII *of Cups*

VIII OF CUPS

Interpretation

Where did that spark go? That *joie de vivre*? The VIII of Cups tells of a deep yearning for passion. Some area of your life has lost a vital zest, and you're thinking about giving up, letting go, and moving on. Take time for deep self-reflection before making any major decisions. Be sure that you're not taking anyone in your life for granted. Remember ideas and goals that you were once excited about. Backtrack a little and rekindle your fire for an old dream. The VIII of Cups says that now's the time to bring some variety and passion back into your life.

Self-Care Card Activities

Mind: Shake things up by signing up for a fun class to learn a new skill, like French cooking or woodworking.

Body: Set aside a few minutes to stretch throughout the day to increase your flexibility, improve your posture, and promote wellness overall.

Spirit: Set yourself up for a great day by listening to uplifting music as you get ready in the morning.

VIII of Cups Reversed

When reversed, the VIII of Cups can indicate that you're coasting through life on autopilot. You've got some sort of big decision to make, and each option comes with its own heaviness. When VIII of Cups presents itself reversed, I recommend pulling a three-card spread for more insight. The first card drawn represents the true nature of Option A. The second card represents the true nature of Option B. The third card is your Advice card. It will give you more clarity on how to decide between the two options.

IX of Cups

Interpretation

Good news: Your wish has been granted! The IX of Cups card is all about abundance, success, and indulging in the sweet fruits of your labor. In a relationship reading, this card indicates that things are moving along swimmingly. You have beautiful compatibility, and you enrich each other's lives tremendously. Now is the time to enjoy yourself. Life is sweet! In a tarot reading that calls for a "yes" or "no" answer, IX of Cups is a definitive "yes!"

Self-Care Card Activities

Mind: Indulge a little. Book a vacation—you've earned it!

Body: Honor and celebrate your body by taking a long, lovely bubble bath with a perfumed, skin-nourishing bath bomb.

Spirit: Switch things up by waking up earlier than you usually do this week. Use the extra time to make yourself a balanced breakfast, do yoga, or set conscious, positive intentions for your day.

IX of Cups Reversed

When reversed, the IX of Cups can indicate that you've taken the card's celebratory upright energy a bit too far. Have you become a little overindulgent? Enjoying luxuries is great, but take care that you're not becoming too materialistic. Did you buy those expensive new shoes because you love them, or just because they'll get lots of attention when shared on social media? Honestly, the reversed IX of Cups can signify that you may have become a little out of touch lately. Remember that you are more than what you own. Reconnecting with your spirit will help shake you from any overly self-indulgent tendencies.

X of Cups

Interpretation

Every time I draw the X of Cups card in a tarot reading, a big smile spreads across my face. In essence, that's what this tarot card is: a big, glowing smile from the cosmos. Lucky stars are shining on you now. The X of Cups represents a blissful, beautiful period in life; everything just feels *right*. In relationship readings, this card represents stable unions that are built on solid foundations. "This relationship is simply meant to be!" proclaims the X of Cups card. The stars have aligned above you.

Self-Care Card Activities

Mind: Be present and take pleasure in every little beautiful thing as self-care. Write nightly in a diary or journal to remember every detail of your day.

Body: Try out a new skincare product, like a deeply hydrating facial serum or nourishing body lotion.

Spirit: Celebrate your accomplishments. Whether you just bought a house, got a promotion, or paid off a loan, take a moment to honor how far you've come. You're doing great!

X of Cups Reversed

The X of Cups card in the reversed position indicates that things are out of sync. As this is a Cups card, the imbalance is probably occurring in a relationship. Have you been struggling to see things eye to eye with a romantic partner? Maybe you've been butting heads with a close friend lately. Be sure that you're communicating well with your loved ones. Be direct about your needs, goals, and expectations. If things still feel off after working on improving communication, it could be time to move on.

Page of Cups

PAGE OF CUPS

Interpretation

The Page of Cups tarot card represents creativity, curiosity, and fresh insight. Sometimes, it also heralds the arrival of a new romantic interest! In fact, this card is often associated with the feeling of being head over heels in love. Have you met someone special recently? This is a lovely period in time for you! The four Page cards in tarot are also divine messengers, so when a Page shows up in a reading, it's likely the universe is trying to communicate with you. Keep an eye out for signs.

Self-Care Card Activities

Mind: Add a few potted plants to your home décor. Choose purifying ones like lady palm or philodendron, which leave the air as revitalized as the Page of Cups has left you.

Body: Switch up your hair care routine by trying a new treatment, like a moisturizing hair mask or stimulating scalp scrub.

Spirit: Reconnect with your intuition by meditating with celestite, a crystal that helps create clear connections with the spiritual world.

Page of Cups Reversed

The Page of Cups card often shows up reversed in a tarot reading when blockages are present. Maybe you want to get started on a creative project or begin a new relationship, but you are caught up in worries about the proverbial "what if?" Work through these issues by remembering your own power. This card may also come up when someone is being a bit immature. Do you know someone who's being really demanding, overly dramatic, or unnecessarily whiny? It's time for them to get it together! If this person is you, recognizing your problematic behavior is the first step.

Knight of Cups

KNIGHT OF CUPS

Interpretation

The Knight of Cups represents the knight-in-shining-armor archetype. Creative, beautiful, and utterly romantic, the Knight of Cups represents someone who's totally ready to sweep you off your feet. The Knight of Cups can show up in a tarot reading when you're craving beauty in your life. Have you been penny-pinching lately, or stuck in an aesthetic rut? The Knight of Cups may indicate that you need to indulge in a few of the things that make life comfortable and beautiful.

Mind: Curate beauty all around you. Buy yourself a bouquet of flowers or a potted plant to liven up your desk at work.

Body: Splurge on a luxe skincare product, like a facial serum, body lotion, or face mask.

Spirit: Write down positive affirmations of self-love and keep them on your bathroom counter or mirror. Say them out loud as you look at yourself in the mirror every morning as a reminder of your own beauty—inside and out.

Knight of Cups Reversed

When reversed, the Knight of Cups card represents someone who is brooding and overly sensitive to the point of being insufferable. *Yikes.* This person storms off to pout when they don't get what they want, when they want it. This reversed position can also indicate someone who is prone to intense jealousy. Pro tip: Don't put up with emotional manipulation or overbearing people! You deserve healthy relationships built on mutual respect. Everyone has bad days, sure, but if someone in your life is embodying the energy of the Knight of Cups reversed consistently, consider limiting time spent with them.

Queen of Cups

QUEEN OF CUPS

Interpretation

The Queen of Cups tarot card embodies a compassionate, open, and emotionally healthy personality archetype. Sometimes when the Queen of Cups card comes up in a tarot reading, it represents a maternal figure in your life. This person has a beautiful, nurturing nature, and is a great caregiver or homemaker. This card can also be a sign that you need to try to be more like the Queen of Cups. Remind yourself that there's strength in being tender. Stay soft, and look after the needs of others—as well as your own.

Self-Care Card Activities

Mind: Create alone time for yourself. Take a bubble bath, go to lunch solo, or snuggle up on your sofa with a new book.

Body: Do you brush your teeth, floss, and get dental checkups as often as your dentist recommends? If not, make a positive change in your dental care routine.

Spirit: Get up early to watch the sun rise and marvel at the beauty of nature.

Queen of Cups Reversed

When reversed, the Queen of Cups indicates that you may have let emotions get the better of you. The energy embodied by this reading takes the idea of wearing your heart on your sleeve to a whole new (problematic) level. Is there someone who's been overstepping your emotional or personal boundaries? The Queen of Cups here serves as a bit of a warning. Take a step back to gain a healthier perspective, and beware of the impulse to lash out emotionally. If a relationship has been feeling smothering or uncomfortably intense, a bit of distance can benefit everyone involved.

King of Cups

KING OF CUPS

Interpretation

The personality archetype represented by the King of Cups is wise, strong, emotionally stable, and a great provider. The King of Cups can represent an authority or paternal figure in your life, or serve as a sign that you need to try a gentler approach to leadership. Now isn't the time for tyranny and barking orders. Your audience will respond better if you approach things with a little more kindness and understanding. The best leaders are compassionate, sensible, and decisive, like the King of Cups.

Self-Care Card Activities

Mind: Evaluate the priorities in your life by making pie charts. How do you divide your time daily? Weekly? Do any of your routines need to change in order to prioritize parts of your life differently?

Body: Focus your exercise routine on building stamina. Try stair climbing, cycling, or weightlifting.

Spirit: Listen to classical music for a relaxing, inspiring break in routine.

King of Cups Reversed

When reversed, the King of Cups symbolizes someone who handles their emotions inappropriately. This person may be vindictive, vengeful, or even emotionally manipulative. If you know someone like this in your life, limit your interactions with them. It may even be time to cut ties and move on. A big part of self-care is recognizing toxic people who consistently exhibit problematic behaviors. Steer clear from them. If you love the person represented by the King of Cups reversed, the situation may be tough to deal with, but you can't let their behavior continue unchecked. Beware of making excuses for this person, and above all, do what's best for you.

Ace of Wands

ACE OF WANDS

Interpretation

Strike while the iron is hot! The Ace of Wands is a card of inspired, focused action. When this tarot card is drawn in a reading, it indicates that now is not the time for hesitation or prolonged planning. If you're starting a new project or journey, the Ace of Wands speaks of the enthusiasm and excitement you're feeling about this new adventure. Don't waste time or energy worrying about potential problems right now. With the Ace of Wands, your ideas are touched with creative brilliance. *Whoa.* So it's time to take those ideas to the next level. Make your move—you've got this!

Self-Care Card Activities

Mind: Learn a new creative skill, like embroidery or knitting.

Body: Fuse fitness and fun by taking a dance class.

Spirit: Promote creativity and new ideas by adorning your office or home work space with bumble bee jasper.

Ace of Wands Reversed

Reversed, the action and enthusiastic momentum embodied by the upright Ace of Wands is blocked. Things aren't going according to plan. To find out what's causing this delay or blockage, pull another tarot card. As the Ace of Wands reversed is a minor arcana, also keep in mind that this issue is temporary. You have what it takes to get out of this little rut and make this venture a success! As self-care, get inspired. Stargaze, and marvel at the vastness of the sky. Go to the ocean, and consider the mystery and majesty of it. The Ace of Wands reversed indicates that you have the potential for greatness. Believe in yourself.

II of Wands

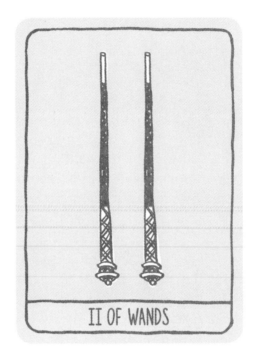

II OF WANDS

Interpretation

Tarot numerology tells us that the II of Wands indicates a choice to be made. There's an element of balance in this decision; it could be that either choice leads to a positive, but very different, outcome. When this card comes up in a reading, an additional three-card spread can be helpful. The first card represents Option A. The second card embodies Option B. The final card is your Advice card, which will give you insight on how to make your decision.

Self-Care Card Activities

Mind: Commit to making your bed every day for a week. It will instantly make the whole room look cleaner, and you just might love the feeling of crawling into a nice, tidy bed so much that you create a lasting habit out of it.

Body: Try exercises that improve balance, like side planks, one-legged squats, and yoga.

Spirit: Reassess your emotional, physical, and personal boundaries. Remember that communicating and enforcing them is essential.

. . . .

II of Wands Reversed

When reversed, II of Wands tells of a decision to be made that may be past due. Is there a choice you've been struggling to make, or maybe just avoiding? This tarot reading indicates that it may be time to get out of your head and seek the opinions of trusted advisors in order to gain some perspective. As self-care, make a coffee date with a friend and dish your drama. Talk over the situation, and discuss all of your options. However, sometimes II of Wands reversed can indicate coercion or manipulation, so take this advice from others with a grain of salt and always go with your gut.

III of Wands

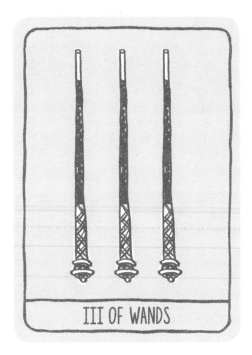

Interpretation

III of Wands often speaks of an exciting creative collaboration. It's a card of friendship, togetherness, and innovative communities. When the III of Wands shows up in a tarot reading, it's a sign to be social. Go out with friends! Spend time with family. Get out of your own head for a while and have a good time. Have you been working on a project with others? This card is a positive sign that it's headed in the right direction. Daydream of all the possibilities now. Who knows what magic the future has in store for you? Also be sure to celebrate all of your successes along the way. You're doing great!

Self-Care Card Activities

Mind: Enjoy the moment! Call up your friends and treat yourselves to a delicious lunch at a trendy restaurant.

Body: Try a fun hula hoop workout.

Spirit: Plan a mini-vacation or weekend getaway. Simply getting out of your normal routine and changing up the scenery will be enough to make you feel rejuvenated.

III of Wands Reversed

When reversed, III of Wands indicates that a once-promising venture has soured. There was a breakdown in a collaboration—maybe communication was poor, or those involved just weren't on the same page. Now is not the time for charging ahead blindly; maintain composure, take a moment to breathe, and reformulate your strategy. Success is still attainable, but your process may need tweaking. Be sure that your goals are sensible during this revamp. III of Wands reversed can also indicate social isolation, so check in with your friends and family as self-care.

IV of Wands

IV OF WANDS

Interpretation

It's time to celebrate! You've completed an important step toward a major goal, so take a moment to pat yourself on the back. You've earned it! The IV of Wands can represent taking the next step in a relationship, hitting an important career or life goal, or even celebrating a birthday. No matter what it is that you're commemorating, the point is that you're moving forward in life. This card often indicates a happy, stable home or partnership. Pause to enjoy the blissful energy of this card, but take care to keep it moving into the future. There are bright blue skies ahead!

Mind: Ask friends for podcast suggestions, and listen to them while you do chores around the house.

Body: Sign up for a yoga class!

Spirit: What are you most thankful for? Make a gratitude list to help you stay mindful and appreciative of all the beauty in your life.

IV of Wands Reversed

Reversed, IV of Wands represents a setback. Have you encountered a bit of bad luck on your way to reaching a goal? Though this obstacle may feel like a big, disappointing problem, know that it's relatively small in the grand scheme of things. After all, the IV of Wands is a minor arcana card, and minor arcana indicate events that are temporary. Put the situation into perspective if you start to feel overwhelmed or discouraged, and tweak your strategy if necessary. Whatever you do, maintain enthusiasm for your vision. This dilemma is just a little bump in the road.

⇒ V of Wands ⇐

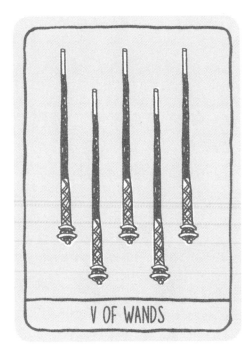

V OF WANDS

Interpretation

V of Wands speaks of conflict and tension. As this is a card within the Wands suit, these conflicts are likely relating to ideas. Have you been butting heads with a loved one or coworker? This card comes as a reminder that you won't always get along with everyone, and that's okay. Sometimes, a little friction can lead to great personal growth. Clear communication is super important right now. It's time for productive, open-minded discussions, rather than combative arguments. Don't lose your cool. Who knows? Everyone involved might learn something from this exchange of ideas!

Self-Care Card Activities

Mind: Reach out to your friends for advice. They can help you put conflicts and situations into a healthy perspective.

Body: Take care of your complexion! Treat yourself to a multistep skincare regimen.

Spirit: Keep a sodalite sphere on your desk at work, or put some sodalite in a centerpiece on your coffee table to promote peaceful interactions, understanding, and harmony.

V of Wands Reversed

V of Wands often shows up reversed in a tarot reading when a potential conflict is being avoided—to someone's detriment. I get it! Disagreements can be super uncomfortable. Arguing isn't fun, and the thought of discussing something major with someone who isn't seeing your point of view can be daunting. Still, turning a blind eye to this situation is helping absolutely no one. V of Wands reversed is your sign to speak up. Find your voice, and use it! Your opinions and feelings are valid and deserve to be expressed.

VI of Wands

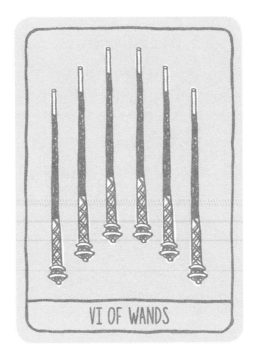

VI OF WANDS

Interpretation

The VI of Wands typically signifies a period of victory. You're being recognized for your accomplishments! Congrats! Now's not the time for humility: You've accomplished something awesome, and you should accept praise for it. Be proud of yourself. Sometimes, VI of Wands comes up in a tarot reading when you're feeling low and in need of a self-confidence boost. This card is a sign to celebrate yourself with positive affirmations. Push self-deprecating, negative thoughts out of your head, and give positivity room to bloom. No matter what's going on in your life, VI of Wands is encouraging and congratulatory. There is so much for you to be happy about; look around and enjoy it.

Self-Care Card Activities

Mind: Note the things that make you happiest. In a fun, brightly colored journal, write down at least one thing that makes you happy each day.

Body: Find a silly vintage workout video and have fun exercising at home.

Spirit: Prevent energy blockages by acknowledging your emotions. Express them in healthy ways, like talking through things in a therapy session.

VI of Wands Reversed

When reversed, VI of Wands represents an ego imbalance. Either you're feeling a major lack of self-confidence, or you've let your ego run away with you. If you're not feeling very confident, try focusing on self-care practices that build you up. Make a list of things you like about yourself, and tape it to your bathroom mirror to read every day. If you're on the other side of the coin, know that while self-confidence is great, it's important to still value the opinions, input, and feelings of people around you.

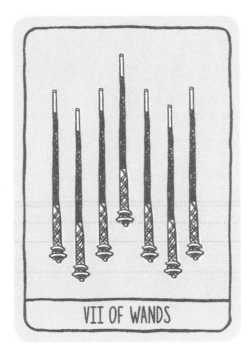

VII OF WANDS

Interpretation

VII of Wands is a tarot card with really defensive energy. You're on guard now. This could be because you're experiencing some degree of competition, or you feel threatened. Know that now is the time to stand your ground; protect what's rightfully yours with vigor. While there's definitely a time and place for diplomacy, this may not be it. VII of Wands reminds you that not everyone involved in this conflict will come out on top—that's simply the nature of it. If someone's standing between you and your success, don't let them push you around. Stand your ground, stay the course, and see your vision through to completion.

Self-Care Card Activities

Mind: Make a change in your nighttime routine to support positive sleeping habits. Try out a relaxing noise machine, make your bed a technology-free zone, or simply commit to going to sleep a little earlier.

Body: Encourage healthier hydration habits. Find a snazzy water bottle and start bringing it with you wherever you go.

Spirit: Prevent energy blockages by speaking up rather than letting things build up under the surface.

VII of Wands Reversed

Reversed, VII of Wands reminds you not to give up. You may be feeling like the underdog in a situation. Maybe you're overwhelmed by pressure from others. Don't let this pressure define you. Stand tall, own your value, and act with confidence. VII of Wands also tells you to avoid the trap of comparing yourself to other people. Unnecessary competition is exhausting. As self-care, limit time spent with people who consistently make you feel bad about yourself.

VIII of Wands

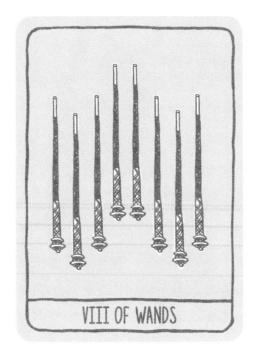

VIII OF WANDS

Interpretation

This tarot card tells you that things are happening quickly now. There's a rush of movement in your life, and while the VIII of Wands indicates that this is a positive thing, it can totally feel overwhelming. You may have just been given a big opportunity or promotion, and you're suddenly finding yourself super busy. Don't let this new, faster pace dizzy you. Instead, embrace the change. Welcome all the activity; meet this movement head-on with enthusiasm, and great things will happen in your life. You'll be rewarded for all your effort!

Self-Care Card Activities

Mind: Create a to-do list and check off items as you go. When you're done with all the tasks on the list, treat yourself!

Body: Make sure to eat healthy foods that will fuel you through this busy period, and remember to take your vitamins!

Spirit: Connect with nature by starting a little herb garden! Nurturing plants can be deeply fulfilling and relaxing—plus, fresh herbs are always great to have on hand.

VIII of Wands Reversed

The energy and fast pace of the VIII of Wands upright is still present when reversed, but you may not be dealing with this sudden rush of activity well. Are you feeling like you're in over your head? Maybe out of your league? You're not! Break tasks down into manageable, bite-sized pieces; be realistic, and keep it simple. When VIII of Wands shows up reversed, it can also indicate that something will be delayed, so prepare for unexpected setbacks. Give yourself extra time to get where you need to go, both physically and metaphysically.

IX of Wands

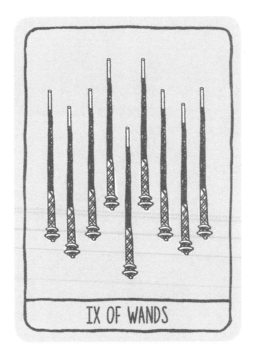

IX OF WANDS

Interpretation

IX of Wands comes to you in a tarot reading when you need to persist. Have you been fighting something in your life? IX of Wands signifies that you're nearing the end of it now. Though the temptation to give up is present, IX of Wands reminds you to have faith in the vision that drives you; the end is in sight and your success is important. Sure, there may be challenges right now, but you've come *so* far! Be courageous and keep going. You've got this.

Self-Care Card Activities

Mind: Is there a friend you haven't spoken to in a little while? Invite them to brunch!

Body: Treat yourself to a spa session, even if you do it yourself at home. You'll feel so refreshed.

Spirit: Give your self-confidence a boost by carrying crystals or stones like bloodstone and green aventurine, which bolster courage and bring success.

IX of Wands Reversed

Reversed, IX of Wands indicates that your defenses are up, potentially to the point of an unhealthy paranoia. Is the world really out to get you, or are you just being cynical? You need a lot of control to feel comfortable, but letting go of it can be rewarding in a lot of ways. Sometimes, IX of Wands is drawn reversed in readings when you're experiencing a lot of setbacks or obstacles and are feeling overwhelmed and discouraged by them. The energy of this card is short-term, so remember that this feeling is temporary. This is the home stretch—don't neglect yourself now! Make time for yourself, and rejuvenate your spirit by booking a spa day.

X of Wands

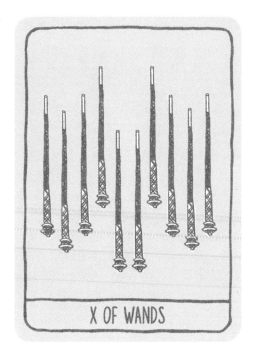

X OF WANDS

Interpretation

The X of Wands indicates that there's a heavy load to bear, and you're feeling weighed down by it. You've had a lot of success, and this comes with a lot of responsibility. Are you getting caught up in the details of all these burdens? Have you become so busy that you've lost sight of your original motivation? X of Wands is a reminder to find your original spark. What vision led you here? What were your motivating dreams? Remember them, and use them to fuel your fire.

Self-Care Card Activities

Mind: Don't take on more work or responsibility than you're comfortably able to. Remember that it's okay to say no.

Body: Combat the side effects of stress by indulging in a deeply moisturizing sheet mask.

Spirit: Explore your astrological birth chart to get to know yourself and your deepest desires better.

X of Wands Reversed

X of Wands reversed tells of an energetic imbalance within your responsibilities. Either you've accepted so much work that you're super stressed and overwhelmed, or you've lost your passion and are avoiding responsibility entirely. Either way, X of Wands reversed indicates that you're feeling unfulfilled in some way. If you're not putting you best effort into your career or a relationship, it could be because you're just not feeling appreciated anymore. Think back to a time when you felt energized and truly happy. Remember how lovely that felt, and chase that feeling. Maybe it's time to turn the page and start a new life chapter. X of Wands reversed confidently says, "Wake yourself up and make a bold change!"

Page of Wands

PAGE OF WANDS

Interpretation

The Page of Wands personality archetype is kind, energetic, and a little naïve in their inexperience. The Page of Wands is effervescent, but not necessarily very efficient, methodical, or responsible. This card represents someone who is absolutely full of bright, optimistic energy. This person is marvelously in touch with their inner child. Sometimes, the Page of Wands drawn in a tarot reading tells you that good news is on the way. As this card is part of the Wands suit, this welcome news likely relates to creativity, expression, or new ideas.

Self-Care Card Activities

Mind: Get inspired! Go to a theater and see a musical or play.

Body: Use a foam roller to release tension in your muscles so there will be plenty of room for the creative juices to flow.

Spirit: Reread your favorite childhood book to spark happy, nostalgic feelings.

Page of Wands Reversed

Reversed, the Page of Wands personality archetype is emotionally immature, irresponsible, and maybe even a bit self-centered. The person represented by this card may easily brainstorm bright, promising ideas but lack the self-discipline to follow through on the practical steps needed to see that vision come to fruition. If this card represents you, focus on incorporating more practicality into your self-care routines. After all, self-care isn't just about bubble baths and positive affirmations! Self-care includes attending to the little tasks that life calls for. Cleaning your house is self-care; paying your bills is self-care. The Page of Wands reminds you not to get so swept up in grand ideas that you neglect your sensibility.

Knight of Wands

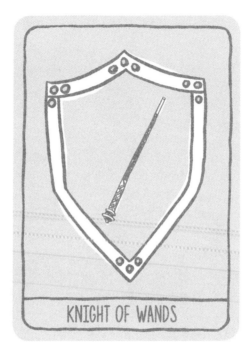

KNIGHT OF WANDS

Interpretation

The Knight of Wands takes the dreamy visions of the Page of Wands and runs with them. The personality archetype embodied by the Knight of Wands is bold, quick-witted, and charming. This person is full of *joie de vivre* and has a fiery passion for life that can't be tamed. Rather than stopping at passion, the Knight of Wands puts action behind their ideas. They love exploring new places and going on adventures. The Knight of Wands daydreams of slaying dragons and rescuing damsels from castles and does their best to make their own life a fairy tale.

Self-Care Card Activities

Mind: Give yourself the room to chase your passions by clearing space in your schedule.

Body: Sleep in. Your body (and mind) will love the extra rest!

Spirit: Practice deep breathing, and take the time to ponder things before responding to a situation or person.

. . . .

Knight of Wands Reversed

The personality archetype depicted by the Knight of Wands in the reversed position is superficial and restless to the point of distraction. They may be moody and prone to throwing tantrums when they don't get what they want precisely when they want it. Reversed, the Knight of Wands represents someone who acts hastily without thinking things through, and this can get them into trouble—or cause them to do things they regret later on. When this card shows up reversed in a tarot reading, it can be a sign that you need to prepare more before taking any action. Be sensible, and keep a rational mind.

Queen of Wands

QUEEN OF WANDS

Interpretation

The Queen of Wands has the sort of decisive spirit that comes with deep, carefully cultivated self-pride. The personality archetype represented by this tarot card is wonderfully confident. They boldly pursue what they want with a mature, focused sort of passion. As such, the Queen of Wands is quite accustomed to getting what they want. When this card is drawn in a tarot reading, be sure to soak up its beautiful energy. Become the Queen of Wands; be bold and courageous in the pursuit of your career and creative goals, and know that you deserve success.

Self-Care Card Activities

Mind: Try out new perfumes or colognes, and choose an invigorating signature scent that will have you feeling confident wherever you go.

Body: Add a little luxury to your hydration habits. Use lemons, limes, and cucumber to enhance your water and add a little pick-me-up, or get creative with herbs like mint, basil, and rosemary.

Spirit: Meditate on the expectations of others and how they differ from your own desires. Use this insight to practice living by your own standards.

. . . .

Queen of Wands Reversed

Reversed, the Queen of Wands feels powerless; they've lost their confidence. They could be dealing with this feeling by becoming very bossy, or by shrinking into a shy wallflower. The person represented by this card may be a tyrannical authority figure in your life, or a power-hungry competitor. When the Queen of Wands reversed appears in a tarot reading, take care to be a little sweeter and more compassionate. Be careful to approach collaborations with social tact and kindness to avoid creating hostility or resentment.

King of Wands

KING OF WANDS

Interpretation

When the King of Wands is drawn in a reading, success is indicated. The King of Wands is a powerful, accomplished leader, and very business savvy. Shrewd and calculating, they naturally command respect. In a reading, this card may indicate that you need to be better at delegating tasks. The time for visionary dreaming is over. Use your fiery leadership skills to see that others implement the structures and rules you create. If you're working on a project now, you're the one who ultimately determines whether or not it will be successful. Trust that you have the knowledge and skill to meet your goals.

Self-Care Card Activities

Mind: For an invigorating boost, buy a citrus-scented candle, or use citrus essential oils in your diffuser.

Body: Give yourself the royal treatment with hydrating eye cream.

Spirit: Connect with crystals that promote peace, understanding, and tenderness, such as prehnite, amazonite, or rose quartz. Sleep with them by your bed, or meditate with them in a quiet place.

King of Wands Reversed

When reversed, the King of Wands tells of a person with poor leadership skills. This person may be tyrannical or dishing out unrealistic goals. They may be a coercive micromanager, or overly critical of everything. The person represented by this card will do *anything* to get what they want. As self-care, be careful to make sure you're not embodying any of these negative traits. If you're in a leadership position, try managing with a kinder approach. Also consider giving back to those less fortunate. Donate to an animal shelter, or volunteer at a soup kitchen to remind yourself of the importance of compassion.

Ace of Swords

ACE OF SWORDS

Interpretation

The Ace of Swords tarot card is embodied by the proverbial *ah-ha*! moment. It heralds breakthroughs, epiphanies, and sudden moments of powerful clarity. Have you been struggling to focus lately? Maybe you've been feeling like you're in a bit of a rut. The Ace of Swords is here to tell you that this period will soon be over. Clarity is here to bring you fresh insight! Be sure to welcome this energy with an open mind.

Self-Care Card Activities

Mind: Now's a great time to finally deep-clean your car. Throw away any garbage, vacuum the seats and floor thoroughly, and wipe down hard surfaces.

Body: Take a self-defense class. No swords needed to find your inner strength.

Spirit: Meditate with aura-cleansing crystals like apatite or selenite for a refreshing energetic boost.

Ace of Swords Reversed

Reversed, the Ace of Swords tarot card indicates that you may be feeling scatterbrained and unable to focus. You may be experiencing a creative block or working very hard at a task without really getting anywhere. The reversed Ace of Swords is a call to slice through this mental fog. Focus your self-care routines on manifesting clarity. Gather an orange candle and crystals that help to promote focus, such as vanadinite, carnelian, and garnet. Sit down in a quiet space, light the candle, and hold the crystals in your hand. Focus your attention on the dancing flame. Whenever your mind begins to wander, catch it, and bring it back to the flame. This practice can help improve your concentration and clear your mind of unnecessary distractions.

II of Swords

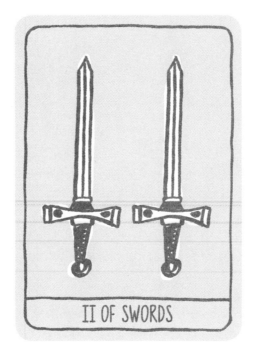

II OF SWORDS

Interpretation

II of Swords usually indicates that there's a tough choice to be made. You're having trouble making this decision, and this could be because you're lacking clarity. You may be stalling, or even avoiding making a decision altogether, but know that you can't do this forever. This dilemma won't magically go away, unfortunately. The solution requires that you take a step back and center yourself so that you can see things more clearly.

Self-Care Card Activities

Mind: Shake up your routines by doing something unexpected! Go on a road trip with no destination, or call up a friend and go see the latest feel-good film.

Body: Treat yourself to comfortable, supportive new shoes. Your feet will thank you—and you'll feel grounded and ready to make that tough decision.

Spirit: For a refreshing, clarifying boost, open your windows and welcome in the breeze.

II of Swords Reversed

Reversed, the II of Swords tarot card can indicate that you're feeling confused and overwhelmed. If you have a decision to make, you've stalled. Maybe you're caught in the middle of an argument between loved ones, or neither of your options seems ideal. No matter what the nature of this predicament is, you feel like you're in the center of a lose-lose scenario. To get yourself out of this sticky situation, follow your intuition. You have all the information you need—all that's left to do is listen to your own inner conscience. What's your gut telling you to do here? If you're still unsure, focus your self-care on activities that help you connect with your sixth sense, such as meditating with amethyst or reciting a mantra like "my intuition is my guide," to open your third eye.

III of Swords

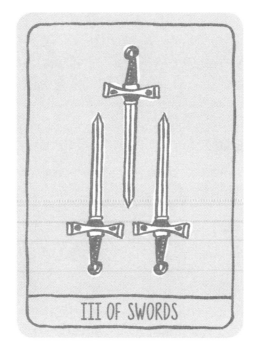

III OF SWORDS

Interpretation

The III of Swords is a pretty intense tarot card to get in a reading. It symbolizes heartache, loss, and emotional upheaval. Has something deeply hurt your feelings? Has a recent breakup left you heartbroken? Whatever's going on in your life, you're definitely feeling emotional pain. The silver lining is that this pain is temporary; this is a transitional period for you. Everyone experiences rough times in their lives, and these situations usually lead to great personal growth. Remember that this heartache won't last forever. The sun will come out again, and things will be okay.

Self-Care Card Activities

Mind: Cancel plans and enjoy a little alone time to recharge your batteries during this emotional time.

Body: Soak up the sun for an instant mood booster. Go to the beach, work outside in your garden, or go for a walk or jog. Just remember to apply sunscreen first!

Spirit: Browse through books online, at a library, or in a bookstore, and read one with a cover you're drawn to, no matter what it's about. The distraction from a tough situation can be quite the mood lifter.

III of Swords Reversed

When reversed, the III of Swords signifies that you're going through a period of deep healing. You've been wounded recently, and your heart is hurting. Take comfort in knowing that things are on the mend. When the III of Swords card is drawn reversed in a tarot reading, it's like a sigh of relief: You've survived that difficult period. The worst of it is over! Surround yourself with comfortable things, like snuggly blankets and warm cups of herbal tea. Be patient with yourself: You're healing.

IV of Swords

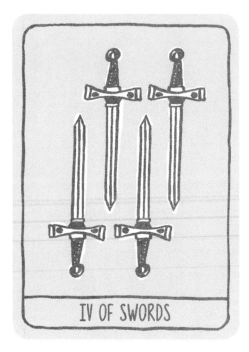

IV OF SWORDS

Interpretation

When the IV of Swords card appears in a tarot reading, it indicates a period of rest. If you've been fighting a bit of a battle lately, the IV of Swords advises you to set aside some time to be alone. Embrace introspection. Carefully analyze the situation or predicament you find yourself in; think about things from every angle, and take time to consider the strategy you're using to reach your goals. Could your plans use some tweaking? Take a step back, and reconsider your path if necessary. The IV of Swords calls for sensibility and reflection.

Self-Care Card Activities

Mind: Recharge and clear jumbled thoughts by hosting a tea party, complete with French macarons and fine china. Pinky up!

Body: Brew a big pot of relaxing herbal tea.

Spirit: Try crystal meditation. Lapis lazuli and amethyst are calming crystals that can help get you into the introspective mood you need to dive deep and recharge.

IV of Swords Reversed

Reversed, the IV of Swords card begs you to chill out. Is there a situation or dilemma in your life that has you feeling frenzied? Panicked, even? Maybe you've been anxious and flustered as a result of this. Impulsivity can lead to mistakes, and you're using up way too much energy being so frantic, so take a step back and breathe. Things probably aren't as dire as they seem. Seek the advice of friends, counselors, therapists, or other trusted individuals to help you gain a more balanced perspective. Remember that you don't need to show up with your sword drawn to every battle!

V of Swords

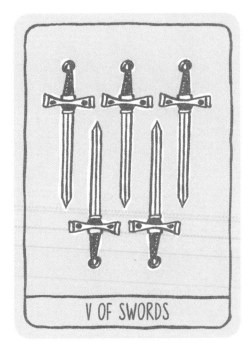

V OF SWORDS

Interpretation

All V tarot cards represent conflict and change in some way, but this particular card also boasts the prideful, intense energy of the Swords suit. So, the V of Swords speaks of really aggressive battles. Those fighting in these battles will do so with teeth and nails. If you've adopted this kind of mentality, the V of Swords can be a sign that it's time for self-reflection. You may have become short-sighted in your pursuit of victory. Have you been hurting someone along the way? The V of Swords also has an element of defeat to it; this is a situation with winners and losers. If you don't rein in your pride and recognize when compromise is called for, the loser could be you.

Self-Care Card Activities

Mind: Organize your thoughts by bullet journaling.

Body: Take a big, deep breath. Exhale slowly.

Spirit: Ask for help when you need it. Be sure to pay it forward by helping someone else out when you're able to.

V of Swords Reversed

V of Swords reversed can indicate that a battle is occurring, but the energy and motivation behind this battle is waning. It's getting old and tiresome, and compromise may now be called for. If you've been fighting with someone, it could be time to concede, or to come to a mutually beneficial agreement. Letting bygones be bygones can be really difficult; still, swallowing your pride and letting this situation go might be the best course of action for everyone involved. Know that you can maintain healthy boundaries while still being civil. Shake hands and move on.

VI of Swords

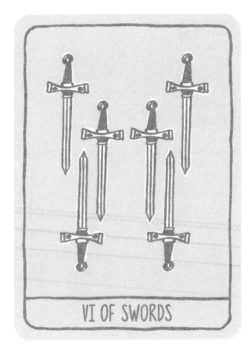

VI OF SWORDS

Interpretation

The VI of Swords card comes up in a tarot reading when it's time to shed old skin to prepare for new growth. Now is your chance to leave something behind and move on. Don't linger on what you're losing; instead, focus your gaze on the bright horizons ahead of you. After all, you're making way for bigger, better things. Is there a friendship that isn't serving you well anymore? Maybe you're moving, and feeling sad about leaving your former home. VI of Swords tells you that change is worth it in the long run. Sometimes, VI of Swords can even indicate actual travel. You could be going on an unexpected trip—be sure to keep your bag packed!

Self-Care Card Activities

Mind: Give yourself a little break from technology by powering down for an hour or two.

Body: Listen to your body's limitations. Don't push workouts beyond what's safe and comfortable.

Spirit: Be gentle with yourself. Be mindful of self-criticisms and remember that you're doing the best you can.

. . . .

VI of Swords Reversed

Reversed, VI of Swords can indicate that you're stuck in a situation you would rather not be in. This has you feeling quite low, both energetically and emotionally. You may be sad, melancholic, or even depressed. What has you down? Are you stuck in the past in some way, refusing to let go and move on? Change is necessary now. You're stuck in a bit of a rut, but the VI of Swords card tells you that this is fixable. Pick yourself up, dust yourself off, and go outside to clear your mind.

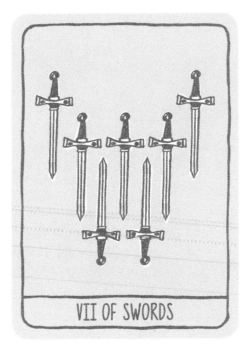

VII OF SWORDS

Interpretation

This tarot card usually signifies a heavy, heartbreaking betrayal. This betrayal may be something you experience, or you could be the one betraying someone else. Remember that whenever you act in nefarious ways, your deeds come back to haunt you. Be sure you're acting in accordance with your conscience to avoid hurting others. If you're not the ne'er-do-well in this situation, the VII of Swords card warns you to keep your defenses up. Be careful whom you trust with personal or confidential information. Don't let yourself become paranoid, but do be cautious.

Self-Care Card Activities

Mind: Ground your mind and calm negative emotions with a good book.

Body: Take a boxing class. The glove might just be mightier than the sword.

Spirit: Keep your energy clean, clear, and protected by listening to energetically cleansing sounds. Singing bowls, bells, and chimes are great for disrupting and driving out negative energy.

VII of Swords Reversed

Have you been trying to lie to yourself? Maybe you're trying to justify resorting to actions that aren't truly in alignment with your values. Have you been keeping things on the up and up lately, or have you been up to no good? Be honest with yourself. You hurt your spirit when you act in ways that aren't in accordance with your inner voice and conscience. You know what you need to do to set things straight. As self-care, be truthful about your intentions. Consider being more up front with people, or make more of an effort to be fair in your business dealings. Getting back in touch with your compassionate side through volunteer work can also help make things right.

VIII of Swords

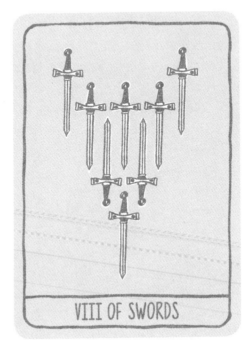

VIII OF SWORDS

Interpretation

The VIII of Swords card presents itself in a tarot reading when you're feeling stuck, trapped, or backed into a corner. Do you feel like you're caught between a rock and a hard place? VIII of Swords is a card with lonesome energy; whatever battle you're fighting, it seems as though you have to do it all alone. You're feeling melancholic, isolated, and maybe even exhausted. But know that all is not lost. As this is a Swords card, the solution to this situation lies in your perception, so try seeing things from a new perspective! You have the strength to fight your way out of this.

Self-Care Card Activities

Mind: Listen to a podcast that expresses an opposing viewpoint. You don't have to agree with them; the goal is to understand where they're coming from.

Body: Get your hands a bit dirty with some volunteer work to bring yourself back to reality.

Spirit: Focus on working through anything that's burdening your soul. Talk it out over coffee with a friend, or book a therapy session.

VIII of Swords Reversed

The VIII of Swords card reversed tells of mental breakthroughs and sudden clarity. You've broken the chains that once weighed you down. Congrats! Now you're using the memory of them to fuel your fire. VIII of Swords reversed is a card of clearheaded perseverance. You may still be fighting a battle, but there's been an upset in the power balance, and you're coming out on top. The clouds are clearing, and the sun is in sight—chase it.

IX of Swords

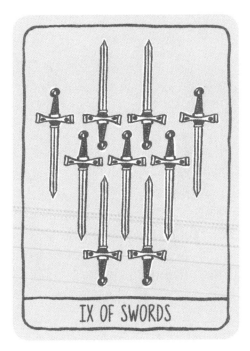

Interpretation

The IX of Swords is a card of intense anxiety. When it comes up in a tarot reading, it represents mental anguish, nightmares, and excessive worry. It often appears in a reading when your anxiety is at its very worst. What has you in this mental state? It is important to reflect on the things that are making you anxious and to work on calming your mind now. Remember that things aren't always as bad as they seem—and they also aren't permanent. Don't let your anxieties ruin the day.

Self-Care Card Activities

Mind: Apply rational thought to your fears. Is what you're anxious about really an issue, or are you just afraid of a vague or unlikely possibility?

Body: Focus on self-care activities that fuel you. Eat a balanced breakfast and remember to take your vitamins.

Spirit: Carry stones that are great for promoting courageous energy, focus, and determination, such as bloodstone and aragonite.

IX of Swords Reversed

Have you recently sought help for anxiety or depression? If so, the IX of Swords card reversed is an indication that you're on the right path. The presence of this reversed card in a tarot reading says that the clouds will soon part and the sun will shine again. If you've been feeling overwhelmed with anxiety, worry, or deep sadness and you haven't sought help, this reading signifies that it's time to do so. The message of the IX of Swords is: "You don't have to go through this alone." Whether you turn to a therapist, a psychiatrist or psychologist, or alternative therapies such as acupuncture or Reiki, proactive measures will benefit your mental health.

X of Swords

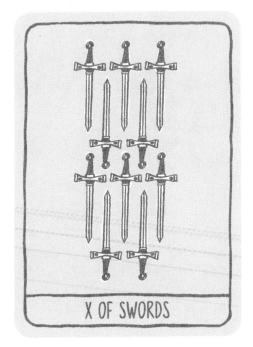

X OF SWORDS

Interpretation

The X of Swords symbolizes an intense, dramatic twist of fate. This can come in the form of an unexpected betrayal, the ending of a close relationship, or other sudden, unforeseen shifts in your life. No matter what specific event this card is referring to in your life, there's an element of finality to it. "The past is over," the X of Swords card is telling you. Allow yourself to fully process the ending you're experiencing, but don't spend too much time dwelling on it, either. Grow from this experience and take stock of all the positives in your life.

Mind: Rearrange your home décor with feng shui to promote a calm, clear mind.

Body: Reduce tension in your body during this uncertain time by using massage balls.

Spirit: If you're having nightmares or trouble sleeping, place selenite, amethyst, or rose quartz by your bed to promote calming, protective energy.

X of Swords Reversed

Has it felt like the world is against you lately? Maybe you feel as though you've been wronged, and you just can't let the situation go. X of Swords comes to you reversed in a tarot reading when you're feeling low. Sometimes, this reading indicates that you could be emotionally stuck in the past. Don't dwell! It's over. The only thing to do now is move forward with your life. Ultimately, the message of the X of Swords reversed is that there are better times ahead, so dream of those bright horizons instead of focusing on what you've lost.

Page of Swords

PAGE OF SWORDS

Interpretation

The Page of Swords tarot card represents someone who is quick-thinking, analytical, and overall very intelligent. Although this person may be emotionally immature, their intellect is nothing short of inspiring. This isn't a card that speaks of hard-earned, cultivated knowledge, however. Rather, it tells of a person who has a natural knack for creative problem-solving. If this tarot card comes forward in a reading that involves a decision to be made, the Page of Swords directs you to steer clear from the path of least resistance. Challenge yourself!

Mind: Try out a few environmentally friendly cleaning products, or make your own! The fresh scents and natural utility will surely calm your mind.

Body: Freshen up your look with an edgy new hairstyle.

Spirit: Send a surprise care package to a long-distance friend. Fill it with skincare items, loose-leaf tea, and a good book.

. . . .

Page of Swords Reversed

The intellect of the upright Page of Swords is still present when the card is reversed, but indicates, frankly, someone who is a bit of an egotistical know-it-all. Do you know someone who likes to put others down to feel superior? Maybe they publicly highlight others' flaws. The Page of Swords reversed thinks they have all the answers to absolutely every question. If you know a person like this, just remember that they have a lot of growing up to do. They're likely an unhappy, insecure, even naïve person. Hopefully they'll get it together, but in the meantime, try to be patient with them while still keeping them at arm's length.

Knight of Swords

KNIGHT OF SWORDS

Interpretation

This tarot card has a lot of swift, powerful energy and movement behind it. Have you been solving problem after problem lately? Have you been charging forward, blasting away obstacles in your path with an impressive amount of focus and drive? If so, this card likely represents you when it comes forward in a tarot reading. The Knight of Swords is decisive, smart, analytical, strategic, and ready to risk it all in the pursuit of a dream or goal.

Mind: Make the best decision by weighing your options with a pros and cons list.

Body: Give yourself a relaxing gua sha massage to increase circulation. You'll feel energized and ready to continue your success streak!

Spirit: Carry garnet with you, as it can help you stay focused on the present. Chasing your dreams is great, but enjoying the moments along the way is important too.

Knight of Swords Reversed

When the Knight of Swords shows up reversed in a tarot reading, it tells you that someone is being totally ruthless in the pursuit of what they want. They will stop at nothing to reach their goal. This card reversed is often a warning. Keep your distance from the person in your life represented by this reversed card because their ambition knows no temperance. While they are intelligent, strategic, and a critical thinker, they can be easily irritated. They may have angry outbursts when things aren't going their way. Don't let this person get a hold on you because you will only be a pawn in their game.

Queen of Swords

QUEEN OF SWORDS

Interpretation

The Queen of Swords represents a personality archetype that is both naturally intelligent and well educated, making them an absolute treasure trove of knowledge and brilliant ideas. The Queen of Swords is logical, sensible, and has an effortless effervescence. They command respect and are a magnetic conversationalist. The Queen of Swords also has a special innate talent: They can see through any form of deceit like no one else. This card represents someone who has a keen sense of justice and truth and little tolerance for actions that don't align with their moral code. Overall, this is a powerful, discerning, and wise person to know.

Self-Care Card Activities

Mind: Carry a pocket-sized notebook with you throughout the day and write down any little questions that come to mind. At the end of the day, spend time searching online for the answers.

Body: Change up your breakfast routine by trying out a healthy new smoothie recipe. The Queen of Swords can certainly get behind this nourishing twist!

Spirit: Connect with whatever divinity you honor, even if it's the divinity within yourself. Try setting aside a few minutes to pray, or practice peaceful meditation or self-reflection.

Queen of Swords Reversed

Reversed, the Queen of Swords card can indicate someone who is jaded, manipulative, and vengeful. This person is an expert saboteur, and their impressive intellect makes them a fearsome opponent. On the lighter side, however, this card may come forward reversed when you've let your emotions get the better of you. Focus on your goals now, and place deliberate action behind them. Don't get swept up in emotional waters, lest you lose sight of your goals.

King of Swords

KING OF SWORDS

Interpretation

The King of Swords is a well-educated authority figure with a strong moral and ethical code—deviation from which isn't often tolerated. This person is strategic to the point of brilliance. A master of cutting to the heart of the situation, the King of Swords represents someone who doesn't appreciate whimsical thinking, emotional pleas, or talking in circles. Sometimes this tarot card is drawn as a sign to ask for the advice of someone impartial, fair, and experienced, such as a lawyer, therapist, or financial advisor.

Self-Care Card Activities

Mind: Organize your thoughts and create a to-do list for putting your latest plan or goal into effect.

Body: Help your inner King of Swords relax by visiting a sauna to release those feel-good endorphins.

Spirit: Listen to the wisdom if others and take their lessons to heart.

King of Swords Reversed

Reversed, the King of Swords represents an authority figure who has absolutely no tolerance for anyone whose views, ideas, or actions don't align with their own. Sometimes, they can take the concept of being stern to the next level, slipping into cruel tendencies. The King of Swords reversed is smart, strategic, and the ultimate gaslighter. This means that they are psychologically manipulative in a way that leaves people questioning their own foundations. If you know someone who embodies the energy of the King of Swords reversed, they are not to be trusted. Distance yourself from them. There's absolutely no reasoning with the King of Swords reversed because they won't ever genuinely listen to your side of things. This single-mindedness can be dangerous, so be smart and avoid this person whenever possible.

Ace of Pentacles

ACE OF PENTACLES

Interpretation

The Ace of Pentacles usually indicates the beginning of financial endeavors. Are you starting a new project at work, or thinking about creating a start-up? This card is a positive sign that the potential to make money is present. Being that it is in the Pentacles suit, the Ace of Pentacles sometimes comes forward when you're feeling grounded and ready to move forward with your life. This could mean that you're preparing to take the next big step in your personal realm, such as getting married, adopting an animal, or buying a house. Whatever endeavors you have on your mind, the potential for success is there.

Self-Care Card Activities

Mind: This is a great time to budget your finances. Exercise impulse restraint, and rein in your spending impulses now.

Body: Focus on nourishment. No matter how busy your day gets, make sure to eat three healthy meals each day.

Spirit: Nurture community—and your endeavors—by collaborating on a fulfilling project with a creative friend or coworker.

Ace of Pentacles Reversed

Reversed, the Ace of Pentacles indicates money lost or ill-spent. Have you been overindulging in luxuries lately? Have these indulgences come at the expense of something else? Maybe you're treating yourself to shopping sprees while there are financial issues to be tended to at home. Part of self-care is making sure your finances are in order. Don't spend money unwisely now. Be cautious with your coin, and make sure that all your bases are covered before you spend on luxuries. The Ace of Pentacles reversed indicates a temptation to spend money with abandon—fight it.

II of Pentacles

II OF PENTACLES

Interpretation

II of Pentacles comes forward in readings when you've got a lot of responsibilities on your plate, usually relating to the home. Are you trying to balance your finances and feeling overwhelmed? Maybe you're stressed out about a meticulous DIY project. The energy for the II of Pentacles tarot card isn't quite that of exasperation, but nearly. You're so busy dealing with day-to-day tasks that you haven't had much time lately for self-care. II of Pentacles is here to remind you that you need time to yourself too.

Mind: Make note of all the tasks you do throughout your typical day. What jobs can you eliminate or cut back on?

Body: Visit a tea shop and try a new, soothing blend.

Spirit: Create time alone for meditation, reflection, and relaxation. Don't get so busy that you neglect your spirit.

II of Pentacles Reversed

Reversed, II of Pentacles is about misspent energy. Have you been dedicating a lot of your time to one project lately, unintentionally neglecting other things? It's time to create more balance in your life. Take a look at how you spend your time throughout the day. Keep track of how much time you spend doing each task, and then make a list of the things that are most important to you. How do these lists align? For example, if spending time with your pet is one of the most important things to you, but you've been spending very little time with them lately, making a conscious effort to give them more of your time will create a fulfilling balance.

III of Pentacles

III OF PENTACLES

Interpretation

Networking is the name of the game here! When the III of Pentacles tarot card comes forward, it's a sign that success won't be reached alone. If you're already working on a project as part of a team, the presence of this card signifies that your endeavor is headed in the right direction. If you're normally a very independent person who likes to do things alone, especially at work, this card could be advising you to work together with others for once. There's a time for working independently, and there's a time for teamwork. This card clearly indicates that this is a time for collaboration.

Self-Care Card Activities

Mind: Work on your communication skills. Attend a public speaking seminar, or find little ways to relate to your coworkers better.

Body: Treat your complexion to an herbal facial steam—team members will say you're positively glowing. Be ready to let them in on the secret.

Spirit: Keep a sodalite crystal on your desk to promote a peaceful environment full of open, clear communication.

III of Pentacles Reversed

Have you been feeling a little lost at work lately? Maybe a project that was once promising has fallen apart due to a lack of cohesive teamwork. The III of Pentacles indicates a lack of essential cooperation, especially relating to the workplace. If you're in a position of authority, now is a great time to boost morale among those you manage because they're feeling dejected and unfocused. Create a teambuilding workshop or plan a fun outing for everyone outside of the office.

IV *of* Pentacles

IV OF PENTACLES

Interpretation

This card has a very protective energy to it. When the IV of Pentacles comes forward in a tarot reading, it indicates that financial security is on your mind. You're saving up and creating a stable foundation on which to build your life. Good for you! Just make sure you're not being too miserly now. Being smart and careful with your money is great, but just make sure to set aside some cash in your budget for fun activities and the little splurges that make life fun. After all, it's all about balance. Work hard and save up, by all means, but don't forget to enjoy yourself.

Self-Care Card Activities

Mind: Let your mind wander a bit. Daydreaming is fun and can be very inspiring.

Body: Budget a nourishing splurge item, like a foot spa or professional massage.

Spirit: Add a potted lucky bamboo or money tree to you home décor. Cultivate its growth to promote abundance and good luck.

IV of Pentacles Reversed

When reversed, IV of Pentacles indicates a problem with the way you're handling your finances. Have you been spending beyond your means lately? Have you become caught up in materialism? Have you come to view your worth as something that's tied to money and objects? On the flip side, maybe you've been pinching pennies to the point of obsession. No matter which extreme direction you're headed in, stop. Pause, and make time for analytical self-reflection. What really makes you happy? Reexamine this relationship with finances and material possessions now so you can get back on track.

V of Pentacles

V OF PENTACLES

Interpretation

The V of Pentacles card comes forward in a tarot reading when you're experiencing instability in your life. As this card is part of the Pentacles suit, this instability likely has to do with finances, careers, or the home. Has your sense of security been shaken recently? Now is a good time to make sure you have what you *need* before indulging in what you *want*. This card can also indicate that you may be getting in the way of your own success. It's important to be your own advocate. And if you need help, ask for it! You are in control—even though you may be feeling powerless at the moment. Know that this feeling is temporary, and achieving stability is possible.

Self-Care Card Activities

Mind: Boost your confidence by shopping for new clothing that makes you feel cool and powerful.

Body: Commit to eating a different superfood (such as kale, blueberries, and avocado) each day for a week.

Spirit: Try creating a little spiritual altar to get back in touch with your soul. Fill it with crystals like celestite, which helps connect to intuition. Place fresh flowers on it, and keep any spiritual books, essential oils, etc. you own there as well.

V of Pentacles Reversed

If you've recently been through a period of financial instability, V of Pentacles reversed may indicate that this time of hardship is coming to an end. You're getting back on track, so stay the course now! If you haven't experienced financial uncertainty, this reversed card could indicate that you're spending too much time worrying about material possessions. Nurture your spiritual self now as self-care.

VI of Pentacles

VI OF PENTACLES

Interpretation

This is a card of giving. If you're in a place where you need help, especially in the financial realm, this card is telling you to ask for it. Now is also the time to accept any help that is offered to you with a grateful heart. And if you're financially successful and in a place of abundance, the VI of Pentacles suggests that you spend some time giving to those less fortunate than you. Donate money, toys, or pet food to your local animal shelter, or give clothing and other necessities to a homeless shelter. Others are in need; exercise compassion, and give with an open heart.

Self-Care Card Activities

Mind: Take time to put away your freshly cleaned clothing properly. A neat, orderly wardrobe will make you feel more put-together.

Body: Give your senses a treat with a new soy candle.

Spirit: Get back in touch with your spirit with a Reiki session or through prayer or meditation. Reconnecting with your higher self will help to create balance and inspire you to share those content, happy vibes with others.

VI of Pentacles Reversed

VI of Pentacles reversed often comes up in a tarot reading when you're neglecting yourself in some way. Do something nice for yourself: Schedule a spa day or salon session. Have you been very worried about financial loss lately? Remember that meaningful self-care doesn't have to cost a lot of money! Bring the spa vibes into your own home with a long, warm bath set to relaxing music. Even if it's something small, it will make you feel a whole lot better!

VII of Pentacles

VII OF PENTACLES

Interpretation

This isn't a tarot card of short-term, instant gratification, but of putting structures in place that will have lasting benefits. The VII of Pentacles is a positive sign that you've planted your seeds well, and so you will have abundance in your future. All you have to do is tend to those seeds now. Soon, you'll be reaping the rewards of all your hard work. Hooray! If you run into little obstacles, persevere! Know that you're on the right path. After all, you're in this for the long haul. Work hard and focus.

Self-Care Card Activities

Mind: Speak positive affirmations aloud. Look in the mirror and say, "I am worthy of abundance. I am powerful. I am loved."

Body: Treat your body to a detoxing bath soak. You've earned it!

Spirit: Be more conscious of the impact your purchases make by buying more environmentally friendly items that aren't animal tested.

VII of Pentacles Reversed

This tarot card reversed can indicate that the success of a current venture will be fleeting—if there's any success at all. If VII of Pentacles comes forward reversed in a tarot reading where you are seeking insight about a project, it indicates that the project may not work out as planned. Now may be time to rethink your plans, tweak your strategies, or even abandon ship altogether. As self-care, make sure you're using your energy wisely, especially where finances are involved. Don't continue to put effort into projects or visions that aren't headed in a positive direction. Take time for some reflection, then make your move.

VIII *of Pentacles*

VIII OF PENTACLES

Interpretation

Often, the VIII of Pentacles comes up in a tarot reading as a positive sign that you're on the right career path. Have you made a professional shift recently? Maybe you've begun a new project or financial venture. This tarot card is one of working hard and mastering skills. You're moving up and creating prosperity for yourself—all thanks to your own efforts. The path to success won't always be easy, but the rewards will be great. Keep your focus, maintain momentum, and you will master your craft.

Self-Care Card Activities

Mind: Exercise your creativity by writing a poem or short story.

Body: Use an essential oil diffuser to fill your living space with invigorating scents, such as citrus or ylang-ylang.

Spirit: Express yourself and release tension by singing your heart out! Put on your favorite song and belt out every word like you mean it.

. . . .

VIII of Pentacles Reversed

VIII of Pentacles reversed can indicate that you're spending your energy un-wisely now. You may be so anxious about a project at work that you're being hypercritical of it. Don't drown in the details. Just breathe; stressing out about your project won't make it more of a success. It's time to tame that perfectionist streak. The VIII of Pentacles may also come forward reversed when you're feeling rather aimless. It may be time to create a lofty financial or professional goal now. Dream big! Aim for the stars to shake yourself out of boredom. Resist the urge to stay comfortable and complacent, and go after something bigger.

IX of Pentacles

IX OF PENTACLES

Interpretation

This is a beautiful tarot card to draw in a reading. The IX of Pentacles signifies abundance, wealth, and deep satisfaction. You're in a place of comfort now, and you've earned it! You're financially secure, and it's time to enjoy the fruits of all your efforts. IX of Pentacles says you've worked hard for all that you have, and now it's time to treat yo' self. Splurge on some luxury items you've had your eye on! Also take a moment to reflect on how far you've come, so you can truly enjoy your wonderful success.

Self-Care Card Activities

Mind: Turn off social media notifications on your phone, set up an out-of-office email auto-reply, and really take time to relax with your luxury purchase(s).

Body: Spray your pillows with a lavender or chamomile pillow spray to promote restful sleep. You'll feel lavish as you recline against these sweet scents!

Spirit: Reduce your environmental impact by buying reusable glass straws. You are living in abundance now—time to switch gears and help out Mother Earth.

IX of Pentacles Reversed

The IX of Pentacles card comes forward reversed in a tarot reading to let you know that you may be working too hard. This card serves as a reminder to slow down every once in a while. Enjoy the abundance in your life! Maybe you've been so caught up in the hustle and bustle of your career that you haven't been making time for much else. I've got two little syllables for you: *vay-cay*. Take a vacation and really pamper yourself! Life is sweet.

X of Pentacles

Interpretation

X of Pentacles is a card of accomplishment. You've done it! You've worked hard, and you're in a place of wealth and abundance now. When this tarot card comes forward in a reading, it signifies the best possible outcome of a situation. All is well with X of Pentacles. This isn't a card of fleeting gratification, either; X of Pentacles speaks of a lasting, hard-earned success. Often X of Pentacles can also signify a happy, stable home life. There's a sense of the importance of family and security tied to this card.

Self-Care Card Activities

Mind: Take a step back and make time for careful self-reflection. A lot of great things have happened—take note of them and of your success.

Body: Use a water bottle with a special compartment for storing crystals so you can soak up good vibes as you hydrate.

Spirit: Watch a sunrise to practice mindfulness for the beauty and abundance around you.

. . . .

X of Pentacles Reversed

Reversed, all that beautiful, bountiful X of Pentacles upright energy gets flipped on its head. This card reversed signifies financial loss, failure, and misaligned personal goals. Are your financial and career goals aligned with what you really value in life? Make sure you're not spending most of your time working at the expense of other things that are important to you, like family. If this card is drawn reversed in a reading about the future of a venture, it is a definite sign that things are not headed in a good direction. When X of Pentacles comes forward reversed, you may have a bit of soul-searching to do.

Page of Pentacles

PAGE OF PENTACLES

Interpretation

The Page of Pentacles symbolizes a person who is eager to learn how to capitalize on their talents. Full of fresh, innovative energy, the Page of Pentacles is a natural visionary. When this tarot card comes forward in a reading, it could be a sign that you're full of innate potential waiting to be explored. So, get to it! Sometimes, the Page of Pentacles tarot card also indicates that a new, lucrative financial opportunity is on the horizon. Have you recently been offered a promotion or new job? Maybe you're debating the pros and cons of an investment opportunity. If so, the Page of Pentacles card is a positive sign.

Mind: Keep the positive vibes coming by taking yourself on a date! Is there a new film out that you're interested in? Go solo, then treat yourself to a lovely candlelit dinner.

Body: Create a comfortable meditation space using plush, supportive cushions and soft lighting.

Spirit: Release your inner visionary. Meditate with tektite crystals to help you dig deep and find hidden truths within yourself.

Page of Pentacles Reversed

Is a project in your life not coming together quite as you had hoped? When the Page of Pentacles is reversed, it can signify an obstacle preventing you from achieving your goals. Remember now that setbacks and mistakes are learning opportunities. Take some time to analyze the situation, but don't dwell on failure or loss for too long. Pick yourself up, and put yourself back out there. Even reversed, the Page of Pentacles holds a lot of potential. Now is the time to be sensible, get excited, and start anew.

Knight of Pentacles

Interpretation

The Knight of Pentacles tarot card is filled with action and forward momentum, especially with regard to careers and finances. The Knight of Pentacles is hardworking, ambitious, and methodical. This tarot card represents someone who isn't much of a dreamer or visionary. Rather, their success comes from following tried-and-true methods with intense focus and dogged determination. When this card comes forward in a tarot reading, it can be a sign that now is not the time to forge new paths. Approach tasks with a healthy amount of sensibility and conservatism.

Self-Care Card Activities

Mind: Reignite your inner spark by infusing your self-care routines with creative self-expression. Sign up for a painting class, or learn how to throw pottery.

Body: Make your morning routine a little more invigorating by using an organic face wash. Choose one with an energizing citrus scent to start your day off with a refreshing boost.

Spirit: Send out some positive vibes for success in your current endeavors by meditating with citrine crystals, saying a prayer, or reciting an empowering mantra.

Knight of Pentacles Reversed

Reversed, the forward momentum embodied by the upright Knight of Pentacles is blocked. This tarot card reversed often represents a figure who is detail-oriented to a fault. Perfectionism can be a great thing, but when taken too far, it can sour success. Take care that you're not micromanaging projects now. Let everyone involved explore and use their own skills to find success. Sometimes, the Knight of Pentacles comes forward reversed when you're feeling stuck in a mundane routine. Challenge yourself to do something fun and unexpected!

Queen of Pentacles

QUEEN OF PENTACLES

Interpretation

The Queen of Pentacles is a nurturing, loving figure who provides stability. Usually this stability is financial, but this tarot card can also refer to emotional stability, or stability within the home. This is a card of financial abundance; the Queen of Pentacles tends to the material needs and wants of loved ones. As such, this card often represents a parent, benefactor, or boss. When the Queen of Pentacles is drawn in a reading, it's often a sign to focus your attention on creating a stable environment within your home—physically and metaphysically.

Mind: Rewatch a film featuring a leading character who inspires you. Find your favorite fictional Queen of Pentacles!

Body: Quality sleep is so important to creating balance and stability. To catch those z's, try a silk sleeping mask.

Spirit: Bring stability into your home by getting your feng shui on! Eliminate household clutter, then thoughtfully add a few potted plants to your space for a boost of refreshing energy.

Queen of Pentacles Reversed

The Queen of Pentacles often comes forward reversed in a tarot reading when you need to focus its nurturing energy on yourself. While the Queen of Pentacles upright symbolizes providing for others, its reversed orientation means that you need to provide for yourself. Focus on becoming financially independent and building success for yourself. Beyond finances, implement comprehensive, healthy self-care practices now that set you up for long-term success. Quash a bad eating habit or adjust your fitness routine. You have what it takes to prosper on your own.

King of Pentacles

KING OF PENTACLES

Interpretation

A disciplined leader, the King of Pentacles is driven, ambitious, and wildly skilled at meeting even their loftiest goals. The success embodied by the King of Pentacles tarot card isn't achieved through sheer luck, however, but by working hard and taking the time to master skills. This tarot card represents someone who is materially successful in a major way. Often, the King of Pentacles card comes forward in a reading when financial or career goals are being met. It symbolizes the acquisition of financial abundance and material success.

Self-Care Card Activities

Mind: Take a methodical, tactful approach to meeting your goals. Map out a detailed plan of action, and charge forward with your head held high.

Body: Plan out your weekly exercises to build a routine that will benefit you long into the future.

Spirit: To motivate yourself and center your energy, place crystals that promote focus and drive, such as aragonite, vanadinite, and garnet on your desk or workspace. Hold them when you need an energetic boost.

. . . .

King of Pentacles Reversed

Reversed, the King of Pentacles can represent one of two personality archetypes: someone obsessed with wealth, status, and power to the point of snobbery and elitism, or someone who overspends, plans finances poorly, or even struggles with poverty. Take care that you're spending money wisely now. Plan out a budget and stick to it! The desire to splurge on luxuries is present when this tarot card is reversed, but remember that exercising a bit of self-restraint will ultimately benefit you way more than wasting money on high-end nonessentials.

PART 3

OPTIMIZING YOUR SELF-CARE

By now you've learned that tarot is an extraordinary tool for self-care. And with a few additional strategies in your reserve, you can unlock the full healing potential of the cards. For example, crystals can amplify the energy manifested during a tarot reading so you are better able to determine the best self-care for you. They also promote elements of self-care in and of themselves, such as improved mood and self-confidence, stress management, creativity, and balanced relationships. Tarot can also be used to explore the shadow-self, which is the subconscious part of you that behaves instinctively. Your shadow-self holds on to toxic conditioning and negative behavior patterns, and you can use tarot to both improve and nourish this self.

In this part, you'll dive a little more deeply into crystals, from how to use them for a beneficial tarot reading to ways to use them for self-care after a tarot reading has finished. Then, you'll discover more about the shadow-self and how to uncover your own inner truths in order to enhance your self-care practices even more. You'll also reveal your personal power card—the tarot card that represents you—and how to use this card to uncover major life lessons and warnings. After traveling through crystals, shadow-selves, and power cards, you'll find out how tarot translates into other parts of your life, including your astrological sign, and how this can lead to better self-care. Tarot's applications to your life are truly limitless! So, are you ready to vibe high with your third eye open? Let's get to it!

Chapter 6

Open Your Third Eye:
Harnessing the Power of Intuition

Have you ever had a gut feeling about something? Have you sensed impending danger or upcoming good news before it actually happened? Or maybe you're able to read other people's vibes easily, picking up on negative emotions or what they are thinking about in a given situation. All of these abilities result from your intuition speaking to you—a "sixth sense," as some people call it. I believe that we all have intuition, but if you don't feel that you're a very perceptive person, don't worry! Your sixth sense can be developed further with practice, and there are lots of ways to help you learn to pay attention to it more closely. Connecting with your intuition can not only make for more insightful, nurturing tarot readings but can also open up your psychic perception—both of the world around you, and of yourself. I've always been a pretty intuitive person, but when I started consciously trying to develop my intuitive skills, *whoa*. Not to be dramatic, but it was as though a veil was lifted, and everything became clearer! Using this heightened perception, you will uncover the best personal care practices for your unique needs and desires. There is truly no limit to where your intuition can take you in your self-care journey.

In this chapter, you'll explore methods for improving your intuitive abilities. From meditating to setting aside time to let your mind play a little through art, you'll soon harness the power of your inner voice. And, speaking of voice, it's also important to recognize the power of your words. After all, they can have a tremendous effect on you! As you dive into your intuition, take care to avoid speaking negativity and manifesting bad vibes. Good vibes only from this point forward!

Methods for Improving Your Intuition

The more time spent connecting with your sixth sense the better because it becomes easier to access your intuition as you familiarize yourself with it. Fortunately, there are a lot of ways to stretch and strengthen intuitive muscles. The following are a few of my favorites; experiment with them to find which methods resonate best with you!

Meditating

Let's face it: Meditation can be a bit intimidating. Personally, I have attention-deficit/hyperactivity disorder (ADHD), and the idea of reaching a calm, meditative state seemed completely unachievable for me at first. I used to feel foolish even *trying* to quiet my mind. Now I meditate almost daily. I promise that it's a lot easier than you might think! Here, I have provided some great tips and tricks to help you get into your own meditative state. You should also keep in mind that you don't need to be a mountaintop meditation master to benefit from this practice. In your modern life, you're constantly bombarded with so many stimuli. Your mind is always on the go, and there are a million scents, sounds, situations, and feelings to sift through: It can get overwhelming at times! Through meditation, you can calm your internal world, sift through everything going on around you, and become more aware of your intuitive voice. It's the perfect self-care practice for your mental health!

To begin meditation, find a quiet, comfortable place to sit alone. Traditional places like a cushion on the floor of a personal space are good, but there are also a number of less conventional meditation spots you can try. For example, I personally like meditating while lounging in a bath. Breathe deeply and steadily. When you have chosen a place to sit, you can either close your eyes or focus them on something entrancing, like the flickering flame of a candle. Next, relax your mind. Thinking of a calming color like a blue-green, minty hue helps me quiet the noise and chaos in my busy brain and gives me a place to center my thoughts. Whenever I find my thoughts beginning to wander a bit, I bring them back to that color. Call to mind whichever color suits you intuitively.

MENTAL SELF-CARE TIP: TRY A MANTRA

Another way people center their minds during meditation, and also bring them back to the present when the urge to daydream pops up, is with a mantra. Some people use traditional mantras, such as "Om" and "Sat nam," when meditating, while others create their own personal mantra. One great mantra when meditating on intuition is "My intuition is my guide."

If you have trouble clearing your mind at first, don't worry! You don't need to reach Nirvana to have a good meditation session. Just do your best. Start by meditating for just a few minutes each day, and work your way up to whatever length of time resonates with you. I try to meditate for five to ten minutes per day, while others aim for half an hour or longer. There are also tons of smartphone apps, websites, and books out there to help you find the best meditation techniques for you, so take some time to explore!

MENTAL SELF-CARE TIP: DIGITALLY DETOX TO CALM YOUR INNER WORLD

Whenever I find myself compulsively checking social media, refreshing my emails, or perusing my friends' profiles, I know it's time to reconnect with myself via a digital detox. Modern technology is so amazing, but it can also be distracting and stressful. I challenge you to turn off your phone. Those social media notifications can wait! Shut your laptop and let it rest. Don't worry about emails right now; power down, and be *present*. Try to notice the little things you've been too preoccupied with technology to enjoy, like the refreshing feeling of the wind in your hair as you walk to the bagel shop for your morning coffee, or the pleasant tinkling of the bell above the door as you enter the salon for a Monday manicure. It's truly amazing how uplifting, clarifying, and stress relieving a simple digital detox can be.

Getting Creative

An easy (and fun!) way to exercise your perceptive muscles is through art. The goal is to access your intuitive mind by exploring an artistic activity that doesn't require much conscious thought. Allow your subconscious to take the reins a little! Personally, I love painting, and creating abstract expressionist artwork allows my mind to travel straight into that intuitive space. Plus, it's so cathartic! I like to start with a big, blank canvas. Then, I simply put paint wherever I feel like putting it. I let myself have fun, and I don't worry about how it will look in the end. If painting isn't really your thing, simple, repetitive art projects can also help you access that calm state of mind. Try knitting, weaving, felting, beading, or embroidery.

Giving Yourself Some Credit

Another way you can develop your intuition is simply by embracing its existence. This seems simple, but it can sometimes be a difficult step. As you grow older, you're often told that cold hard facts are the only things you should focus on, and that things like emotions and gut instincts get in the way of thinking logically. But it's totally possible to be rational, sensible, and *also* intuitive. It's all about striking a balance. So, the time has come to stop denying your intuition. When you get a gut feeling, don't try to dismiss it as silly. Act on it, and take note of how often these feelings are spot-on. Track your hunches in a journal to see any patterns and watch the progress of your intuitive growth over time. I'm willing to bet that you're already more intuitive than you give yourself credit for. Embracing your sixth sense will give it room to blossom.

. . . .

Spiritual Self-Care Activity: Enchant an Object with Empowering Vibes

For even more confidence in exercising your intuition, you can "enchant" an object. This means that you imbue that object with specific energy that you can access every time you use it. Here's an easy spell to enchant an object with energy that makes you feel confident as you continue on your self-care journey.

Items Needed:

- 1 white candle

- 1 clear quartz point

- The object to be enchanted (a piece of jewelry, a coin, a crystal that's special to you, etc.)

Instructions:

1. Light the candle and place the clear quartz point between you and the candle, directing its energy toward you.

2. Hold the object to be enchanted firmly in your hands.

3. Now concentrate on manifesting the energy you want to enchant it with. It may help you to think of a time you felt very powerful and confident. Remember that feeling, and bring it into the present. Feel your chest swell with pride and your posture straighten with confidence.

4. When you feel ready, imagine that manifested energy flowing from you into the object you are holding. The energy is trapped there now, pulsating and glowing. Now every time you come into contact with the object, you'll get a boosting jolt of that powerful energy.

5. To end the spell, blow out the candle. Recharge the object as needed by performing the spell again.

Snoozing Your Way Into Self-Discovery

Dreams can deliver all kinds of messages. Often, they can involve symbolic imagery, acts, or archetypes that relate to issues your subconscious wants you to address. Some people also believe that spiritual entities can communicate with you more easily while you're in a slumbering state. What colors, scents, themes, actions, and imagery have stood out to you in your dreams? Is there a dream you have had more than once? What emotions come up during a dream? How do those emotions carry over into the real world when you wake up? Asking yourself these types of questions can help you uncover what insights your dreams hold for you, and what lies in your subconscious mind.

There are many books and online resources that offer dream interpretations, but keep in mind that interpretations can vary from source to source. Ultimately, it is up to those flexing intuitive muscles to decode what your own dreams mean for you. You can also speak with a spiritual professional for help in understanding a dream and how you can apply its meaning to your waking life. Different cultures and religions also interpret dreams differently, so consider seeking insight from sources relevant to your own traditions and beliefs. Shamans, pastors, psychics, priests, and coven leaders can all be particularly great resources to help you figure out what your dreams are trying to tell you. Consider keeping a dream journal to help you remember details and track any patterns that occur in your dreams.

Physical Self-Care Activity: Manifest a Sweet Slumber

Trouble getting to sleep or staying asleep? This exercise can help you calm restless, tense, or anxious thoughts and get rid of any negative energy you may have manifested over the course of the day, so you can have a refreshing night of uninterrupted sleep. It's also a great spell to use if you've been having nightmares or anxiety-inducing dreams.

Items Needed:

- 1 lighter or box of matches
- 1 dried bundle sage
- 1 small fire-safe container with a lid
- 1 selenite crystal
- 1 amethyst crystal

Instructions:

1. Begin by burning the sage in your fire-safe container. Let the gentle smoke waft throughout your bedroom, cleansing the space of any negative energy. You don't have to burn the entire bundle, either: Just creating a bit of smoke is enough to purify the energy in the room. The rest of the sage can be saved for future cleansings.

2. Place the spiritually cleansing selenite and sweet-dream-inducing amethyst on your bedside table.

3. Say the following incantation out loud: "Bad vibes, dark dreams, stay far from me. I'll have only light here while I sleep."

4. Cover the fire-safe container to put out the burning sage.

5. Now slip into bed and rest easily, knowing your sleep will be peaceful.

Chapter 7

Get Your Sparkle On:
Enhancing Tarot Readings with Crystals

Ah, crystals. Honestly, I'm absolutely obsessed with them. I have crystal facial rollers, candle holders, coasters, and trays. Even my glass water bottle has a special compartment that holds crystals to infuse my drinking water with good energy. I keep a few crystals in the glove compartment of my car, some in my purse, and I wear crystals daily in the form of necklaces, rings, bracelets, and earrings. Like I said: I'm *obsessed*. Why? Because crystals are an amazing aid in self-care. Not only do they enhance tarot readings so you can glean greater insights into what kinds of self-care you need at a given time and what current self-care practices may not be serving you as well as they could, but they are also a form of self-care in and of themselves! Each crystal has unique healing properties that can promote self-care in one or all of the three main areas of mind, body, and soul.

In this chapter, you'll explore popular crystals for optimizing your self-care before, during, and after tarot readings. From rose quartz to amethyst, these beautiful crystals will soon become staples in your tarot self-care routines, and you may even feel inspired to bring them into other self-care practices as well. Let's dive in!

Must-Have Crystals

There are some crystals everyone can benefit from having, regardless of their personal self-care journey. I like to collect multiple shapes and forms of each crystal because the shape can alter the way the crystal gives off energy. For example, crystals polished into a spherical shape give off balanced energy that can really fill a room. Crystal points are used for focusing and directing energy toward a specific purpose. Tumbled crystals or crystals left in their raw, natural state are what I recommend to people who are just starting to experiment with them. They're generally the least expensive shapes available, and they can be used in all sorts of self-care practices. So, whether you're already a crystal connoisseur or you're totally new to this, the following section has you covered.

Rose Quartz for Self-Love

Rose quartz is a tremendously popular crystal, and there's a reason for its popularity: Its vibes have multiple benefits and are absolutely enchanting. A lovely pink color, rose quartz gives off gentle, loving vibes. It's a powerful crystal for cultivating self-love and promoting harmonious environments. Use this crystal in tarot readings that have to do with romantic relationships, friendships, or manifesting a balanced, positive mindset.

Jet for Renewed Vibes

Jet is a variety of coal that has light, uplifting, refreshing vibes. It's energetically cleansing, as well as protective. Jet acts as a sort of metaphysical filter, absorbing negative energy like a sponge to purify a space. Use it during tarot readings as protection against negativity. As it soaks up bad vibes, it has to be cleansed often. To do this, jet can be buried in dirt overnight, passed through the smoke of burning sage or palo santo, or placed beside a crystal with cleansing properties, like selenite.

Selenite for Deep Cleansing

Ah, selenite: It's a metaphysical breath of fresh air! Selenite is one of few crystals that actually cleanse the energy of other crystals and stones. Beyond that, selenite can also purify the vibes of objects and even auras. It's often sold in plate form, so you can rest objects, crystals, and stones on top of it for energetic purification. It is also commonly sold in wand shapes that can be passed over objects for a cleansing boost. Store your tarot deck with selenite to keep the deck's energy squeaky clean and ready for action. As part of your spiritual self-care routine, you can also cleanse your aura by holding selenite while meditating.

Clear Quartz for Energy Amplification

Simply put, clear quartz is dynamite at amplifying energy. When placed beside another crystal, it boosts the healing properties of that crystal, making it a staple in both self-care and your tarot toolbox. Use clear quartz during tarot readings to enhance the energy of the cards (and therefore the lessons and self-care insights you glean from them), or boost the properties of the other crystals and stones involved in the reading. Clear quartz comes in many forms, including the popular elestial clear quartz. This variation is extremely helpful in self-care that focuses on building good habits and unlearning negative behaviors.

Amethyst for Calm Communication

Amethyst is a calming crystal that promotes harmonious communication. Meditating with it before a tarot reading can help you access your intuitive abilities in order to better interpret the cards. As further self-care, you can also meditate with this crystal after arguments to dispel tension. Amethyst is also known for cultivating creativity and promoting sweet dreams. Use it during tarot readings focused on creative pursuits, or keep an amethyst cluster by your bed to ward off nightmares.

MENTAL SELF-CARE TIP:
PLAN A TAROT DATE WITH A FRIEND

Take a tip from the harmonious amethyst by spending time with a friend—and the cards! Bring your tarot deck to brunch, or read tarot in a park over a picnic lunch together. It's a great way to bond over themes and lessons from the cards while nourishing your relationship. Pro tip: Consider taking some selenite with you to spiritually cleanse the deck between spreads. To do this, pass the selenite over the deck a few times, or let the selenite rest on top of the deck while you order another round of coffees.

Exploring Crystal Energy Grids

During a tarot reading, you can amp up the powers of your crystals even more by setting them up in energy grids. There are a few main types of energy grids you can use, depending on the reading you are doing:

- **Elemental.** In this grid, arrange your crystals from each of the five elements (Earth, Water, Fire, Air, and Spirit) so that each one is in the cardinal direction of its element. Have you been feeling a little off-center? Maybe you've been feeling very emotional, or having trouble making decisions based on compassion. This crystal grid works so well to align and balance personal energy. It can make you feel grounded (Earth), motivated (Air), passionate (Fire), emotionally balanced (Water), and personally aligned (Spirit).

- **Sacred Geometric.** This grid is created by setting up crystals in specific geometric patterns. These patterns are based on the idea that there is inherent, sacred divinity in the shapes and patterns found in nature. Do you feel disconnected from the energetic flow of the natural world? Are you feeling insignificant or unsupported? Use crystal grids based on sacred geometry to tap into the intricate magic of universal energy. Sacred geometry crystal gridding will remind you of the interconnectedness of all life, help you feel more in tune with the natural world, and remind you that the universe has your back.

- **Intuitively Created Grids.** In this crystal grid, you follow intuition to place your chosen crystals. Popular ways of intuitively creating crystal grids is to use a central stone that holds the base energy you would like to manifest. Then surround the central stone with other crystals that enhance or complement its energy. This type of crystal gridding can be used for virtually any purpose. Are you feeling unmotivated? Try creating an intuitive grid using aragonite, ruby, and garnet. Are you looking to manifest good luck and positive energy? Create a grid using pyrite, jade, and green aventurine. If you're interested in manifesting your own personal power, choose crystals you feel intuitively drawn to (I usually use elestial quartz, dogtooth calcite, and natural zircon) and create a grid with them.

You can find inspiration for setting up your own intuitive crystal grids online. Be sure to experiment with the different types of grids to discover which ones may be helpful in your own tarot readings and self-care practices.

. . . .

Spiritual Self-Care Activity: Protect Your Home from Bad Vibes

While many people may ask that you take your shoes off at the front door, I have a different request of those who enter my home: that they remove their bad vibes. How? Simply by passing the purifying crystal grid I have set up year-round by my front door. The grid acts as a sort of filter for the energy that passes through, so people are cleansed of bad vibes as they come into my home. This grid includes selenite and jet—and it's easy to make for energy purification in your own home!

Items Needed:
- 1 jet tumble, egg, or sphere
- 4 sticks selenite
- 7 clear quartz points

Instructions:
1. Create a clear space to set up the crystal grid, preferably by the main entrance of your home.
2. Begin by placing the jet in the center of the space.
3. Place the sticks of selenite around the jet in four directions. I like to use a compass and go by the cardinal directions.
4. Place the seven clear quartz points just outside the selenite sticks at even intervals.

As a weekly or monthly ritual (depending on the amount of traffic through your home), burn dried sage or palo santo over the grid to give it an energetic boost. Everyone who stops by will enter and leave feeling positive and empowered. And you will avoid absorbing any negative vibes from guests.

Pairing Tarot with High-Vibe Crystals

Now that you've learned about popular crystals and crystal grids, it's time to take a look at just how to implement these powerful tools in tarot readings. Crystals can be used throughout the entire process of tarot, from before you begin a reading to after the reading is finished. Using crystals in tarot will help you better understand what lessons, warnings, and themes the cards contain so you can use those messages to cultivate the best self-care practices for you. Let's explore the full tarot-crystal process further!

Crystal Prep Work

Before diving into a tarot reading, it's important to prepare your mind so that you will be more receptive to the information that the cards have to offer. To do this, you can meditate with crystals and stones associated with enhancing intuition, such as celestite, amethyst, apatite, and spirit quartz. Also consider setting up a protective crystal grid to ensure that no entities or energies are able to affect the tarot reading unless they are specifically invited into the process. To do this, gather crystals and stones that are spiritually grounding and great for energy protection, such as black tourmaline, jet, onyx, obsidian, hematite, and labradorite. Place them around you in a circle, or set them down in each of the four cardinal directions. The energy of the crystals and stones will radiate around you to ward off any uninvited energy or bad vibes as you prepare to read the cards.

Lights, Crystals, Action

During a tarot reading, you can use specific crystals to both encourage deeper insights into a card drawn and manifest a desired outcome related to that reading and the specific card(s) drawn. For example, when doing a romantic relationship reading, having rose quartz or carnelian on hand can kick-start the fortune of the cards you draw. During a reading about a current dilemma in your life, keeping crystals such as celestite, tektites, and apatite nearby can promote deeper insights from the reading so you are better able to work through this tough time and come out the other end stronger for it! You can simply place the crystals near the deck or hold them in one hand as you draw and interpret cards with the other.

Between Card Movements

Clear quartz is a must-have for me during tarot readings because it's so great at amplifying energy. Not only does it enhance the benefits of the other crystals being used, but it can also bolster any energy the tarot cards may give off during readings. This makes it easier for your intuitive sense to pick up on any messages the cards may be trying to deliver. To amplify the energy of tarot readings, keep clear quartz on top of the tarot deck whenever you're not actively shuffling or drawing cards. You can also put clear quartz directly on top of individual tarot cards after they've been drawn to boost their energy.

SPIRITUAL SELF-CARE TIP: USE CLEAR QUARTZ TO BOOST POSITIVE TAROT READINGS

Clear quartz is especially great for boosting the energy of tarot cards with very positive interpretations, such as The Empress, The Sun, and minor arcana cards numbered X. To boost a positive card with clear quartz, place the crystal directly on top of the positive card that has been drawn. Take time to reflect on the meaning of the card. Soak up and enjoy its sweet vibes!

Back on Earth

After a tarot reading, you can bring your mind back down to the physical realm using stones that are known to be energetically grounding. Smoky quartz, black tourmaline, and hematite are great for this purpose, but they can be a little too energetically heavy and intense for some people, especially tarot beginners. My very favorite, more user-friendly grounding stones are jet and petrified wood. Grounding crystals help to quiet the third eye a bit and bring focus back to your physical reality after a tarot reading. This practice will allow you to smoothly transition from the deep dive into your thoughts to fully participating in the present. Keep the crystal in your pocket as you go about the rest of your day, or wear a necklace that features a grounding stone.

Mental Self-Care Activity: Create an Evening Ritual

Evenings can be a sacred time. As the sun dips low and the tarot cards have been put away, you wind yourself down and spend time getting into the mindset for sleep. The habits you form in the evening can have lasting effects on your sleep patterns, mood, and life overall, so it's important that you create and follow through on rituals that help you get the restful sleep you need. Here's how I use crystals (and lovely scents!) to infuse my own evening ritual with a bit of magic—whether you have trouble falling asleep, staying asleep, or getting yourself into the relaxed mindset for bed, give it a try.

Items Needed:

- Crystals to promote restful sleep, such as rose quartz, amethyst, and labradorite
- Physical self-care items you use before bed, such as a nightly skincare regimen, toothbrush and toothpaste, etc.
- A calming essential oil diffuser or pillow mist such as lavender, chamomile, or sage

Instructions:

1. Begin by gathering your crystals and meditating with them for a few minutes to start the process of calming down from a busy day. As you meditate, breathe deeply and slowly.
2. When you feel ready, perform your nightly physical self-care routine. Wash your face, use your skincare regimen, and brush your teeth.
3. Place the crystals by your bed and turn on your calming essential oil diffuser or mist your pillow with the pillow spray.
4. Set your phone at a distance to resist the urge to start scrolling through social media.
5. Lie back in bed, and go to sleep knowing you're being cared for by the loving vibes of your crystals.

Chapter 8

Dive Deep:
Using Tarot for Self-Exploration

Now that you've navigated the cards, stretched your intuitive muscles, and boosted your readings with crystals, it's time to get even more real with yourself. An essential part of self-care is recognizing your shortcomings. Yes, really! You have to transform your negative behavior patterns into better ones by digging deep to uncover the root of your thoughts and actions, so you can implement new behaviors and practices that are beneficial to your growth and success, rather than detrimental. And tarot is your ticket into this deep self-exploration. More specifically, tarot cards that come up reversed in readings (often called "reversals") hold a wealth of information relating to the ways in which you can improve. No worries or disappointments here, though: Everyone has flaws. Addressing these negative behaviors, thoughts, and tendencies is worth it. After all, you can't vibe high in the light without acknowledging your personal shadow.

In this chapter, you'll discover this shadow, referred to as your "shadow-self." You'll explore the relationship between your shadow-self and tarot reversals, and find out how to use these reversed tarot cards for self-care. You'll also learn how to track your journey through tarot self-care using journaling, and how this practice is not only cathartic but also beneficial to your growth. A special self-care activity will direct you through the steps of creating this personalized tarot journal—but first, let's get to know your shadow-self.

Introducing the Shadow-Self

Everyone has a shadow-self. The shadow-self is the primal part of you that's responsible for your instincts. It's where you hold trauma, and it's the driving force behind problematic behaviors, such as lashing out in anger, being greedy or too selfish, etc. The shadow-self is reactive and wild.

While all of this may seem negative, the shadow-self is not inherently bad. Everyone is made up of both shadow and light. Many people try to stomp on their shadow-selves, thinking this will keep them in the light. While focusing exclusively on light and repressing shadow may sound like a great idea in theory, personal growth doesn't happen by ignoring the areas where you may need improvement. The truth is that everyone has some negative behavior or conditioning to unlearn, or a deeply rooted issue to work through. Everyone has personal baggage to unpack, and ignoring this fact won't get you anywhere.

Taking the time to work with your shadow-self is an important part of self-care. Through shadow work, you not only heal deep hurts and toxic tendencies, but you also become a more conscientious, balanced human being overall. It can be a difficult and bumpy road through shadow work, but fortunately you have a great tool at your disposal: tarot! In the following sections, you'll learn more about using tarot to explore and improve your shadow-self.

. . . .

Spiritual Self-Care Activity:
Explore Your Shadow-Self Using the Major Arcana

The major arcana can teach you many meaningful, deep lessons about your shadow-self. I like to do this particular exercise just before my monthly therapy sessions, to get me in the mood for exploring the ways in which I can improve as a person.

Items Needed:

- Crystals that aid in shadow work, such as indigo gabbro and elestial quartz
- The major arcana cards from a tarot deck

Instructions:

1. Begin by meditating with the crystals you've gathered. Hold them as you focus your mind on your shadow-self energy.

2. Place the crystals nearby and shuffle your major arcana cards. As you shuffle, ask the tarot cards, "What lesson does my shadow-self need to learn to become balanced?"

3. Draw a card. Ask yourself what major life lesson is embodied by this card. What can you learn from it? How can you work on using its message to create balance in your life? Refer to Chapter 4 for more information on the card you have drawn and what it may be trying to tell you now.

Tarot Reversals and Shadow Work

When reversed cards are drawn in tarot readings, they usually indicate the presence of some kind of imbalance that needs to be corrected—an imbalance often connected to your shadow-self. For example, the Queen of Wands upright is a celebrated, creative personality archetype that moves through life with enviable beauty and grace. When reversed, however, the Queen of Wands represents a personality archetype that feels powerless. Often, the Queen of Wands reversed reacts to these feelings inappropriately by either lashing out in frustration or by totally shutting down emotionally. The negative ways in which the Queen of Wands reversed reacts to feelings of powerlessness can be interpreted as shadow-self behaviors: Something under the surface has caused them to react on instinct. Drawing the Queen of Wands reversed during a tarot reading can be a sign to take care that you're not exhibiting these sorts of impulsive, reactive behaviors. It's a call to dig deeply inside yourself to find the root cause of what has you feeling powerless so that you can work through the problem and restore balance within yourself and your life.

PHYSICAL SELF-CARE TIP:
FIND POWER IN YOUR WORKOUT ROUTINE

Take a tip from the reversed Queen of Wands: Remind yourself just how powerful you are through an invigorating combat workout such as kickboxing or karate. Not only will your body thank you for the exercise, but you'll also walk away with a refreshed feeling of empowerment.

When a reversed tarot card is drawn in a reading, reflect on your own actions and energy. Question yourself. What is the meaning of this tarot card when reversed? Are you feeling or behaving in a way that resonates with the energy of this card? How can you use this insight to behave or express yourself in healthier ways? How can you grow from the message of this card? Return to Part 2 for more information on what a certain card means when reversed, and what insights it can offer into your current shadow-self.

Journal It Out

Journaling about your adventures in tarot is a great way to track trends in your readings, access your intuition, and do some shadow work. There are also lots of different ways to journal with tarot! Some people like to keep online journals, while others prefer to write about their experiences in dreamy, giant leather tomes. A simple notebook will do just fine, really, but take a look through different diaries, sketchbooks, or even field notes to find one that strikes you. Some people also like to write with a special or sacred writing implement when journaling about their tarot practices. I prefer felt-tip pens in colors that correspond to the nature of each tarot reading (see Chapter 1 for magical color correspondences), but others use markers, watercolors, colored pencils, etc. Choose the medium that feels right to you!

Tracking Tarot Reversals As Shadow Work

Detailing reversed card readings in your tarot journal is a great way to work through and keep track of the shadow-self lessons each card may be trying to tell you. For example, maybe you drew the V of Swords tarot card reversed. In your journal, you would then write a description of the reversal's general meaning (be sure to include the date the card was drawn). In this case, V of Swords reversed indicates a battle or disagreement that needs to come to an end. You can then apply this message to yourself by pondering areas of friction within your life. Maybe you and a friend have been terse with each other lately, and as you think about it, you realize that your egos are involved. In your journal, you would make note of this current disagreement below the card description, and then apply the card's message to this disagreement. Your shadow-self is involved in this fight because your ego is running away with you, and it's time for this battle to end. V of Swords reversed is telling you to humble yourself a little, check your ego, and talk with your friend as an equal to overcome this friction. All of this insight should be written down in your journal, so you can fully acknowledge this area where you need to improve and jump-start the journey into that shadow work. I also find it helpful to boost the energy of reversals using crystals related to shadow work (nuummite and elestial quartz), placing the crystals on the reversed cards after they are drawn. Give it a try!

Journaling Beyond the Shadow-Self

Maybe your current self-care journey through tarot doesn't involve as much shadow work—or it does, but you are also looking to find your inner voice, tap into your intuition, express yourself creatively, or track your experiences through a broader lens. In this case, there are a few other methods of tarot journaling that can help you navigate your unique personal needs. Take a look at the following types of tarot journaling to discover which one(s) may be helpful to you now.

STREAM OF CONSCIOUSNESS TAROT JOURNALING

This method of tarot journaling is a great option for those looking to use tarot to really connect with their inner voice. In this method, you simply draw a tarot card and freewrite about it. What mental images does the card conjure? For example, does The Empress make you think of roses growing in the sunshine? Maybe The World card reminds you of sandalwood and bergamot scents. Does The Tower make you feel a bit uncomfortable, or even queasy? Write down the things you mentally associate with the tarot card you draw. The writing process should flow easily in this journaling style. Don't put too much conscious thought into what you're writing, how it might sound if read aloud, or if you've spelled things correctly. The product of this method doesn't necessarily have to be clear, or even make sense; it is meant to open your mind. Through stream of consciousness tarot journaling, you can find valuable, deep inspiration hidden within your own psyche!

Art Journaling with Tarot

If you are artistic, this method is especially for you! To make a tarot-themed art journal, begin by drawing a tarot card in a sketchbook. Then, start creating a collage or larger art piece based on the energy invoked by this card. Cut out photos from magazines to paste on the page, or use watercolors to make an abstract expressionist work of art! Add stickers, gems, or other embellishments. You can even use scissors to cut the journal page into a shape that resonates with the energy of the card you drew. Does The Hermit tarot card make you think of deep blue hues and matte finishes? Maybe The Sun card reminds you of sparkly stick-on rhinestones and warm shades of orange. Express yourself and your own unique view of the card. This will help you bond with your tarot deck and connect deeply with your own intuition.

Life Application Tarot Journaling

If you're looking to keep track of your tarot journey in a more straight-forward, organized way, this method could be for you. To start, choose a tarot spread, draw your cards, and write down or illustrate the cards that come forward. Describe how you interpret this spread, and how it applies to your own life. Ask yourself questions to help prompt you as you write. What messages do these cards have for you? How does the meaning of this tarot spread apply to you emotionally? Spiritually? Which people in your life may be represented by any court cards that come forward? What do these court cards say about these people and their relationship with you? Journaling this way can help you notice any trends over time in themes, lessons, and warnings within the cards. Beyond that, it can enable you to make sense of past tarot readings that might not have resonated at the time they were drawn. Sometimes, time needs to pass before a tarot reading makes sense.

. . . .

Spiritual Self-Care Activity: Give Your Tarot Journal Good Vibes

Tarot journals can be deeply personal objects that you connect with on many different levels. I blessed mine with a simple spell to promote creativity, clarity, and a connection with my inner divinity. Writing in my tarot journal is cathartic, and it brings my intuitive mind to the forefront, so marking it as a sacred object makes the whole process of journaling feel more magical, powerful, and productive. Follow the steps below to bless your own journal.

Items Needed:
- 1 pyrite crystal (creativity)
- 1 celestite crystal (connection to the divine)
- 1 selenite crystal (clarity)
- Your tarot journal
- 1 white candle

Instructions:
1. Begin by placing the crystals on top of your tarot journal.
2. Light the candle.
3. With your feet flat on the ground, meditate with both of your palms on the journal. Focus on generating energy and sending it into the journal through your palms. If visualization helps you, imagine white energy flowing up from the ground, through your body, and out into the journal through your palms. Imagine energy flowing from the crystals into the tarot journal, imbuing it with their own special brands of magic.
4. Say the following phrase, your palms still on the journal: "This tarot journal is sacred. It provides me with clarity. It provides me with insight. It provides me with light."
5. When you intuitively feel finished, blow out the candle to signify the end of the spell.

Chapter 9

Own Your Potential: Embracing Your Personal Power Tarot Card

Have you noticed one tarot card in particular that keeps coming forward during your readings? Or does one card perhaps seem to stand out to you more than others? Maybe you feel a sort of kinship with a personality archetype represented by the romantic Knight of Cups, or the hopeful spirit of The Star speaks to you on a deep level. If so, it's possible that you may have already discovered your own personal power tarot card. A personal power tarot card can be quite the inspiring, insightful gem of wisdom. It represents you during a tarot reading, and it resonates with your own personal brands of magic and energy. It can tell you about your shadow-self, reveal your strengths and weaknesses, and offer instructive guidance on how to make progress along your self-care journey.

In this chapter, you'll learn about different methods that can be used to discover your own personal power card. You'll also explore ways to interpret the warnings and lessons revealed by power cards, and how this information can aid in better self-care. You'll also read about each of the twelve signs of the zodiac, which are traditionally associated with the major arcana. Each sign and its accompanying major arcana card will offer you even more self-care practices for your unique needs. So, ready to discover which personal power tarot card is yours? Let's get to it!

Discovering Your Power Card

The Queen of Swords is my personal power tarot card. I discovered it by keeping track of cards that came forward during my tarot sessions in my tarot journal. Over a period of months, I noticed that the Queen of Swords kept popping up in readings, and I realized through my journal insights that this card was representing me in each instance. Following this gut feeling, I went to a professional spiritualist for a tarot reading and channeling session. She drew tarot cards for me, and laid them out on the table between us in a complex spread. Can you guess which tarot card ended up in the very center of this arrangement, representing me? Yes, it was the Queen of Swords!

QUEEN OF SWORDS

You don't have to visit a medium or professional tarot reader to discover your power card, however. The following are other DIY ways to do so on your own. Give them a try!

Ask the Cards

So, you want to know which tarot card is your personal power card? Just ask! That is, ask your tarot deck which card embodies your own traits, behaviors, strengths, and weaknesses, and see which tarot card comes forward. To do this, you should first cleanse your space in your preferred way, whether it's by using the crystal selenite, spraying a purifying essential oil mist, or burning sacred flora. When your space is energetically clean, sit down with your tarot deck, and really focus on manifesting your energy. When you feel aligned and powerful, shuffle the deck. As you shuffle, ask which tarot card is representative of you overall, then draw. Which tarot card came forward? The result may surprise you!

Physical Self-Care Activity: Move Your Body to a Power Card June

Through all of the spiritual and mental work involved in discovering and interpreting your power card, it can be easy to forget the "body" portion of self-care. Use this activity to get your blood pumping and revitalize your physical self-care routines.

Items Needed:

- Your power card
- Your phone, laptop, or whatever you use to listen to music

Instructions:

1. First, look at your power card. How does it make you feel? What is the mood of the card—joyful? Strong? Rebellious?
2. Once you've thought about the emotions linked to your power card, set them to music! Pick a favorite song that matches the energy of your card.
3. Now start dancing! Move to the tune of the song—and your power card.

Notice Tarot Trends

Tarot journaling is a great way to notice trends in specific cards drawn over time. Try keeping track of what cards come forward in your tarot readings, and see if one card shows up more often than any others. If you often draw tarot spreads that involve a placement representative of yourself, look for trends in them. Does one card come forward multiple times in that same placement? If so, this is your personal power tarot card! For more tarot journaling inspiration and information, refer to Chapter 8.

Use Your Intuition

Some people simply recognize their personal power tarot card intuitively! Consider the court cards of each suit, as well as the major arcana. Is there one card in particular that you feel an intuitive connection with? Maybe you're a romantic idealist like the Knight of Cups. Perhaps you feel deeply connected to nature like The Empress. Meditate on this topic. As you dive into your intuition, ask which tarot card represents your very best self, and which tarot card, when reversed, may indicate your shadow-self. This could be your personal power card.

MENTAL SELF-CARE TIP:
DISPLAY YOUR POWER CARD FOR A SELF-CONFIDENCE BOOST

Remind yourself of your own potential for greatness by displaying your power card prominently in your home! I found an artist who made a print of my personal power card that I keep on my vanity. Seeing it every morning as I get ready for the day reminds me of what a powerful, capable person I can be. When you're not using your tarot deck, keep your power card on a mirror in your bathroom or bedroom, or display it in your workspace.

Interpreting the Lessons and Warnings of Your Power Card

Upright, your personal power card represents your best self. It tells of your strengths, goals, and overall nature. When reversed, your power card can offer you glimpses into shadow-self behaviors and personality traits you may be prone to. While upright power cards give you an idea of what you're like at your very best, reversed power cards often tell of personal shadow-self traits you need to watch out for. You can use these insights to focus on areas that could use improvement, and where you might be in need of a little self-care.

For example, my personal power card is the Queen of Swords. When reversed, this card indicates emotional detachment and a cold nature. I take this reversal as a warning not to become like the reversed Queen of Swords. Because of this, I'm conscious of my shadow-self tendency to emotionally check out of situations that involve conflict or friction, and I'm careful to focus my mental self-care practices on maintaining a compassionate, open heart. As part of this self-care, I spend time with loved ones and offer up help to anyone I think might need some assistance.

. . . .

Mental Self-Care Activity: Write a Poem Inspired by Your Personal Power Card

Get your creative vibes flowing and connect more deeply to your power card by writing a poem about it! It doesn't have to be formal or follow a set poem formulation: It can be as structured or as free-flowing as you would like! I recommend handwriting the poem as opposed to typing it up initially because there's something intimate and intentional about writing with pen and paper. Here's how to begin:

Items Needed:
- Your personal power tarot card
- 1 clear quartz crystal
- A pen and piece of paper

Instructions:

1. Place your personal power card on your workspace.

2. Place the clear quartz on top of your power card to amplify its energy.

3. Ruminate on the card for a while. What are the qualities and personality traits embodied by it? What are its lessons? Its warnings? How do you personally identify with the symbolism of the card?

4. Use these insights as inspiration for your poem. Write until you feel that you've connected with the energy of the card and embodied its vibes in your poem.

5. Keep the poem in your tarot journal, or frame it and place it where you can see it regularly.

Taking Tarot to the Stars

Traditionally, both tarot and astrology are known as forms of divination, but their applications can go far beyond just seeing into a possible future. Did you know that these divination arts can be used together for self-care? Each of the twelve signs of the Western zodiac is associated with a tarot card from the major arcana. These cards represent the overall energy of each sign and offer insights into your strengths and weaknesses, in addition to pointing you toward what self-care practices can be most beneficial for you. So, let's take a look at your zodiac sign's tarot card!

Aries (March 21–April 19): The Emperor

Aries is a dominant, logical, assertive sign, which means it is perfectly represented by The Emperor tarot card. Reversed, The Emperor can indicate an Aries shadow-self tendency to become unfocused and scattered, and to clash with authority figures.

SPIRITUAL SELF-CARE TIP

There is strength in being tender-hearted, Aries! You don't need to draw your sword and attend every single battle you're invited to. Connect with your inner softness by regularly meditating with rose quartz and moonstone.

Taurus (April 20–May 20): The Hierophant

The Hierophant loves traditions, structures, and tried-and-true methods for getting things done, which makes it the perfect tarot card to represent hardworking, stable Taurus. Reversed, The Hierophant symbolizes the Taurean tendency to become stubborn and resistant to change.

PHYSICAL SELF-CARE TIP

I know this may be a hard lesson to learn, Taurus, but deviating from the norm can actually be great for you! You love your routines, but welcoming changes can make you a more well-rounded, well-adjusted person. Go on an impromptu adventure! Try a nature hike, and choose a new trail that may be a little challenging for you. An invigorating workout outdoors is just the thing to make you feel aligned, confident, and ready for change.

Gemini (May 21–June 20): The Lovers

The Lovers is a tarot card of choices and duality, which is why it represents the Gemini nature so well. Gemini is social, flirtatious, and loves making connections with a variety of different personalities from all walks of life. Reversed, this tarot card represents the Gemini struggle in coming to definitive decisions.

SPIRITUAL SELF-CARE TIP

Center your energy through crystal meditation whenever you're faced with polarizing choices or feelings, sweet Gemini. This will help you discover your true feelings and come to the best decision for you. Protective crystals with heavy vibes like tourmaline and hematite might be too much for your airy, carefree nature, so try connecting with grounding crystals and stones that have lighter vibes, such as smoky quartz, jet, and petrified wood.

Cancer (June 21–July 22): The Chariot

Those born under the sign of Cancer are highly intuitive, persistent, and loyal people. These traits correspond perfectly to the motivated energy of The Chariot tarot card. Reversed, The Chariot speaks to the Cancer tendency to be uncomfortable with letting go of control.

MENTAL SELF-CARE TIP

Find balance in your life by loosening the reins a little, Cancer! Micromanaging every little detail of your life won't lead to more stability, after all, and demanding so much control will only stress you out. Use calming essential oils like lavender and chamomile in a diffuser, and focus on calm, slow, deep breathing. You deserve to rest and relax!

Leo (July 23–August 22): Strength

Bold, assertive, and kind, Leo is represented by the tarot card Strength. Leos can be showy and flashy, but their hearts are tender and compassionate. Reversed, Strength represents the Leo shadow-self tendency to find themselves in power struggles.

PHYSICAL SELF-CARE TIP

Lovely lion, you don't have to bare your fangs at every little thing that causes some friction in your life. Choose your battles wisely, and spend your energy in productive ways. Take a high-intensity workout class, or try a new physical activity, like boxing or indoor rock climbing. Expending a lot of energy physically will help relieve any frustration you may be feeling so you're clearheaded and ready for your next big idea.

Virgo (August 23–September 22): The Hermit

The Hermit tarot card represents Virgo's intensely analytical, introspective nature. Virgo, like The Hermit, is a detail-oriented perfectionist who usually prefers solitary work to collaborations. Reversed, The Hermit tells of the Virgo shadow-self tendency to isolate themselves. People born under this sign sometimes get so swept up in their own thoughts that they can become a little out of touch.

PHYSICAL SELF-CARE TIP

Virgo, you love to work hard and burn the candle from both ends to make sure that no detail is overlooked, but it's important to make time for yourself every now and then! Yoga or Pilates can help you feel energetically aligned and physically strong. Set aside time to turn notifications off on your phone, ignore your work emails, and allow yourself to be fully present for a great session. With increased flexibility, a stronger core, and a clear mind, you'll be able to dive back into work feeling refreshed and capable.

Libra (September 23–October 22): Justice

Justice is the perfect tarot card to represent the zodiac sign of Libra. Moderate and kind, Libras are known for having a keen sense of right and wrong, and they thrive when there is a fair balance in all areas of their lives. Reversed, the Justice tarot card represents Libras' tendency to avoid friction at all costs. The peacekeepers of the zodiac, Libras have a natural aversion to conflict.

PHYSICAL SELF-CARE TIP

Power struggles and disagreements are often uncomfortable to address, but sometimes it's necessary to take a stand and speak your mind, fair Libra—even if a few feathers are ruffled in the process. To help you find the strength and confidence to say what's on your mind, get into physical strength training! Pumping iron and doing leg press workouts will make you feel powerful and ready to be truly heard.

Scorpio (October 23–November 21): Death

Death is a commonly misunderstood tarot card, and its corresponding zodiac sign, Scorpio, is often perceived as being just as mysterious. Scorpios naturally embrace personal transformations with grace, which is the very essence of the Death tarot card. Reversed, Death represents the Scorpio tendency to be a bit reluctant to move on from things, especially when emotions are involved.

MENTAL SELF-CARE TIP

When you connect with people, you connect deeply, dear Scorpio. You're fiercely loyal, and these attachments can be difficult to sever if they become unhealthy. Still, it's important to recognize when relationships really aren't serving you well anymore. As self-care, set boundaries, and make sure to enforce them. Anyone who doesn't respect them has to go. Your devotion is precious—make sure you're giving it to worthy people.

Sagittarius (November 22–December 21): Temperance

The Temperance tarot card corresponds perfectly to the zodiac sign Sagittarius. Temperance is a high-minded card, and this nods to Sagittarius's philosophical, worldly views and ideas. Sagittarians are full of expansive, abundant energy, and they want to experience absolutely everything life has to offer. As a result, the Sagittarian shadow-self tendency to overindulge is represented by Temperance reversed.

PHYSICAL SELF-CARE TIP

Take a lesson from the Temperance tarot card, Sagittarius, and realize how much better your life is overall when you work to cultivate a deep sense of balance. As self-care, take a long look at your wellness. Are there areas of your physical care that are a little unbalanced lately? Sagittarians naturally have a dreamy, spontaneous spirit. While you're planning grand adventures and racing off on impromptu trips, keep your feet on the ground by eating healthy foods, adjusting your workout routines as necessary, and scheduling regular checkups with doctors.

Capricorn (December 22–January 19): The Devil

The Devil is the tarot card associated with Capricorn. Capricorns have a keen sense of justice, fairness, and duty. As such, they are naturally aware of their shadow-selves, as represented by The Devil in the upright position. Like the two loosely shackled figures featured on traditional Devil cards, Capricorns always have personal power, even when it may seem otherwise. Their sheer determination can get them out of any sticky situation, which is signified by The Devil tarot card reversed.

MENTAL SELF-CARE TIP

Don't be so hard on yourself, Capricorn! Life is difficult, and everyone has both shadow and light. Work on your shadow-self, of course, but don't beat yourself up for having areas where you can use a bit of improvement. As self-care, write a list of personal affirmations. Keep it on your bedside table or vanity mirror to remind yourself of your best qualities, and read it out loud whenever you're feeling like you're not good enough. You totally are!

Aquarius (January 20–February 18): The Star

Aquarius is the visionary dreamer of the zodiac, making it perfectly represented by the hopeful energy of The Star tarot card. Aquarius and The Star are both inspiring figures that encourage people to daydream about all the possibilities. Reversed, The Star alludes to the Aquarian shadow-self tendency to sometimes feel hopeless and lost.

SPIRITUAL SELF-CARE TIP

Dream your wild dream, Aquarius, but don't get so swept up in your visions that you lose touch with practicality. Your rose-colored glasses are beautiful, but remember to take them off every now and then to retain a sense of balance and sensibility. Keep your feet on the ground by meditating with protective, grounding crystals, like obsidian, black tourmaline, or hematite. Keep them with you (in a bag or pocket, or as jewelry) on days when you really have to stay level-headed and get things done.

Pisces (February 19–March 20): The Moon

The Moon tarot card is all about diving deep below the surface to get to the soft, tender heart of things, making it the perfect match for the emotional nature of Pisces. Pisces dislikes superficiality and thrives in uncharted waters. Reversed, The Moon represents the Piscean tendency to get caught up in worrisome what-ifs and become anxious.

SPIRITUAL SELF-CARE TIP

The loving Piscean heart is beautiful and something to be treasured, but you often get swept up in emotions and ideas. Other people's baggage, moods, and grief can affect you on a deep level. Setting emotional boundaries will help protect your heart. Book a rejuvenating Reiki session to balance your energy. You'll feel more centered and in control.

Chapter 10

So, What's Next?
Further Tarot Lessons for Everyday Self-Care

Tarot reading can seem like a magical practice for peering into the future, but as you have come to find out, it has very real, everyday-life applications too. Tarot can help you when you're down in the dumps. It can give you fresh, new perspectives and valuable advice, and help you to shake yourself out of creative blocks. Bad day at work? Draw a tarot spread to find out where things went wrong. New love interest? Lay out a tarot spread to find out who they really are and where things are heading. Tough decision to make? Turn to the cards for help deciding. Just bored at a coffee shop with a friend? Keep a tarot deck in your bag so you can bust it out when you need a fun activity. I turn to tarot whenever I need situational advice or insight into a dilemma, and whenever I want to dig into my subconscious mind to discover my true goals, motivations, and internal conflicts. I even use tarot in my spellwork and witchcraft.

In this chapter, you'll discover more ways to bring the nurturing magic of tarot into your daily life. From helping you overcome negativity, stagnant energy, and creative blocks, to being your own personal life coach, tarot has your back every step of the way in your journey through self-care. You'll also find out about a few divine tools for self-care *beyond* the cards, from chakras to palmistry. Let's dive in!

Using Tarot to Transcend the Doldrums

Part of self-care is acknowledging your bad days. It would be absolutely marvelous if life could be sunshine and rainbows all day, every day, but that's just not the nature of the world you live in; every now and then, storms brew. Sometimes you feel bogged down by worries and stressors. Deadlines loom overhead, work piles up, and life just feels *heavy*. Whenever I feel a little down, or I'm stuck in the doldrums (that spell of melancholy and listlessness everyone falls into from time to time), I use tarot as self-care to see things from new perspectives and get me into a more positive mindset. In the following sections, I have shared my tips for using tarot to pull yourself out of the doldrums.

Staying Hopeful with The Star

In the story of The Fool's Journey (detailed in Chapter 2), The Fool falls asleep in The Tower, which is struck by lightning in the night. It crumbles, and The Fool barely escapes. Just after this period of unexpected darkness and destruction, The Fool looks skyward and sees The Star. This reminds them that there is always hope, even in the bleakest of situations. After a bit of rest and self-reflection, The Fool carries on their journey to enlightenment, and eventually reaches brighter, happier days. Take this story to heart, and remember it whenever you feel sad. During difficult times in life, pull out The Star card from your tarot deck and place it prominently on your vanity, bathroom mirror, bedside table, or work desk. Use this visual to remember that there are better times ahead. Bad days don't last forever!

PHYSICAL SELF-CARE TIP:
ENHANCE YOUR SHINE WITH A FUN WORKOUT

Using The Sun's energy, bring some more light into your day with a workout that has you energized and smiling. Dance workouts like Zumba and Jazzercise get your heart pumping while making you laugh as you attempt to follow fast rhythms and funny movements with a class.

Using Tarot As Your Personal Life Coach

Tarot can help you find meaningful steps to take throughout your life—just like a life coach! Whenever you're faced with a difficult time, for example, ask your tarot deck for advice through questions like "How can I resolve this conflict?" or "What lessons do I need to learn in order to move on from this period?" If the answers the cards provide seem unclear, don't be shy about drawing more cards for clarity. The honest insight that comes forward may surprise you. Whether the answers received are spiritual messages from a higher power or come from your own inner consciousness, the uplifting, inspirational effect tarot readings can have in times of stress or sadness is magnificent.

Banishing Creative Blocks

Creative blocks can be frustrating to say the least. Maybe you've been struggling to flesh out a short story, or you've been finding it difficult to express yourself through your usual artistic medium, like painting, drawing, or knitting. Everyone experiences these creative blocks from time to time, and getting out of a block can seem almost impossible when you're in the thick of it. I have a little tip for you, straight from the tarot cards: The next time you're in a mental rut, try opening your third eye. Bust out your sage! Clear the air of any negativity with some selenite or palo santo. Turn on your essential oil diffuser and deeply breathe in energizing citrus scents. Check in with your chakras, and give each of them a little TLC with crystals or sound therapy. Then, give *yourself* a little cosmic therapy with a tarot spread. Let go of your frustration and stress, and focus on the tactile experience of shuffling, dealing, and turning the cards. Trust them to guide you back into alignment. You'll be amazed by the brilliant new ideas you may find yourself coming up with when you take the time to re-center yourself!

More Divine Practices for Self-Care

Tarot is a beautiful tool for self-care in and of itself, but it also serves as a centerpiece from which other divine forms of personal care stem. As you have learned in previous chapters, part of the magic of tarot is that it informs and aids in these other modes of self-care, advising you on which practices you might benefit from focusing on. My own nourishing rituals include tasseography (the art of reading tea leaves, as you explored in Part 1), and palmistry, with a focus on chiromancy over chirognomy. I also use swinging crystal pendulums not only for divination but also to seek guidance and advice, and to practice astrology and crystal healing (examined more in-depth earlier in this Part). I both casually and ritualistically balance my chakras, and I perform self-empowering spellwork as well. All of these tools have helped me to cultivate myself into a happier, more mindful person.

I encourage you to explore these divine practices more on your own if they interest you! The following sections provide an overview of each one (note that you will find more information on tasseography in Chapter 1, crystal healing in Chapter 7, and astrology in Chapter 9). Check them out, and pursue any methods that ring true with you personally.

Palmistry

Palmistry is based on the characteristics of the hand and markings of the palm. It's divided into two main arts: chiromancy and chirognomy. Chiromancy focuses on interpreting the symbolism of the lines and markings etched into the palm. Chirognomy involves studying the other characteristics of the hand, such as subtle skin color changes, the individual shapes of the fingers, palm, and hand, and the texture variations found on the hand.

The ways of interpreting these characteristics vary from culture to culture, but in my practice, the dominant hand tells of past, present, and future events and themes in a person's life, while the nondominant hand tells of destiny and integral personality traits. Practicing palmistry can help you better develop your sense of personal identity, and may also make you feel like the universe has your back, even in difficult times. If a tarot reading has indicated that you need to gain more self-confidence, dive deep into your consciousness, or ride out a current or imminent challenge, palm reading may be a helpful next step.

Pendulum Dowsing

Pendulum dowsing is the practice of using a swinging pendulum to receive answers to questions. Some people tap into their intuition when using a pendulum and think of pendulum dowsing as a way to focus their own energy to discover answers, while others believe spiritual beings control the pendulum and guide it to responses. Personally, I don't invite deities or spirits into my divination practices, so I use my pendulum to channel answers from my own energy.

Pendulum dowsing is super simple and easy to do! In many cases, you lay out a special cloth or board with possible answers written on it, and hover the pendulum over it while focusing on your query. The direction and way the pendulum moves over the cloth or board helps to interpret a possible answer. It doesn't typically give the sort of deep insight that tarot reading offers, but it's great for helping you make decisions that the cards have advised that you make one way or the other.

· ·

Spiritual Self-Care Activity: Use a Pendulum to Check In with Your Chakras

I use my pendulum whenever I need direct, clear answers to specific questions, but pendulums can also be used to gauge the energy flowing through your chakras. This activity will give you insights about the health of your chakras and alert you to any energy blockages so that you can then focus your attention on correcting them.

Items Needed:

- A pendulum
- A comfortable surface to lie down on
- A friend

Instructions:

1. Begin by meditating with your pendulum. Hold it in both hands and focus on manifesting and centering your energy.
2. When you feel ready, lie down flat on your back with your arms at your sides.
3. Have your friend hover the pendulum over each of your seven chakras individually. Note the movement of the pendulum as it hovers over the energy centers. If it moves clockwise, energy is flowing freely. Counter-clockwise movement or a total lack of movement indicates that the chakra is blocked or out of balance.

Restoring balance to your chakras through meditation, sound therapies, crystal healing, or Reiki will leave you feeling confident, centered, and powerful!

· ·

Chakra Energy Work

Chakras are energy centers throughout the body. Bringing balance to them leaves you in a place of inner peace, control, and personal power. There are seven main energy centers in total (root, sacral, solar plexus, heart, throat, third eye, and crown), and each one is thought to control different aspects of your wellness (physical vitality and security; emotions and relationships; confidence and self-acceptance; love and personal growth; creativity and self-expression; mental clarity and intuition; and spirituality and your connection to the divine, respectively). When an energetic blockage develops in a chakra, you can feel sluggish or out of balance. Fortunately, there are many ways to get rid of blockages and bring your chakras back into alignment, such as meditating, practicing yoga, visiting a Reiki practitioner, using crystal healing, or applying chakra-specific sound therapies. Beyond pendulum dousing, you can use your tarot deck to check in on your chakras or seek advice on how to clear any blockages.

Self-Empowering Spellwork

As part of my self-care routine, I practice spellwork. Essentially, this involves collecting specific herbs, crystals, candles, and other items during certain lunar phases or astrological movements, and combining them with magical intent to promote personal wellness. My spellwork makes me feel more confident, in control, centered, and in tune with the natural rhythms of the universe. You can use your tarot deck to inform on spellwork that might be beneficial to your own wellness! Simply ask the cards for insight on this divine self-care—whether it is on the practice as a whole, or on certain elements of it such as crystals or candles—and interpret what they have to say.

Vibing High with Self-Care

At the end of the day, discovering and embracing your own authenticity is at the heart of self-care. Through tarot and the other divine practices you've discovered in these pages, you can unlock the best self-care routines for you, ultimately manifesting your best self and living a deeply fulfilling life. And that is where the real magic lies.

Index